Takahiko Mukoyama
Tetsuo Takashima
with studio ET CETERA

GENTOSHA

PREVIOUSLY IN THE BIG FAT CAT SERIES
~これまでの BIG FAT CAT シリーズ~

「パイ・ヘヴン」――パイの天国。はじめて持った自分の店に、青年がつけた名前だった。でも、そこは天国にはほど遠い場所だった。
　青年の名はエド・ウィッシュボーン。パイ職人になる夢をかなえるため、人口八千人の小さな町、エヴァーヴィルへとやってきた。お店を無事オープンへとこぎつけて、すべては順調に見えたが、なぜかお客さんはよりつかず、連日の閑古鳥。唯一やってくる者といえば、大きな太った野良猫がブルーベリー・パイを盗みに来るだけ。先行きは暗かったが、生来の楽天家のエドはなんとかなるだろうと気楽に構えていた。
　しかし、そんなある日、町の再開発計画によって、エドの店はブルドーザーにつぶされてしまう。エドは一夜にしてすべてを失い、バッグひとつと、いつしか住み着いてしまった猫を抱えて路頭に迷うことになった。(『ビッグ・ファット・キャットとマスタード・パイ』)

夕暮れの町を茫然と歩くエドと猫。その目にとまったのはニュー・エヴァーヴィル・モールの新店舗募集の看板だった。ほかに頼る当てもないエドは、いちかばちかモールのオーナーのところへ面接に向かう。しかし、そこにはすでに先客がいた。エドと同じぐらいの年齢で、やはりパイの店を経営している大富豪の息子、ジェレミー・ライトフット・ジュニアである。しかし、二人の大きな違いは、ジェレミーの方は大型パイ・チェーン店の「ゾンビ・パイ」で成功を収めていることだった。勝ち目のない戦いに、エドはその場から逃げ出そうとするが、オーナーはエドのまっすぐな人柄を気に入り、チャンスをくれた。「今日の閉店時間までに来月分の賃貸費を支払ってくれれば、店舗のひとつを君に任せよう」

　信じられない思いで、エドは銀行へと走った。貯金をすべて降ろし、モールへと引き返してくるエド。しかし、モールに入る直前、黒いリムジンがお金の入ったバッグをひったくり、エドをはねて、彼方へと消え去ってしまう。猫と共に──。(『ビッグ・ファット・キャット、街へ行く』)

Billy Bob

The Owner of the New Everville Mall

Jeremy Lightfoot Jr.

もうろうとする意識の中、町を彷徨うエド。寒さと疲れで意識を失い、気がつくと見たことのない通りの一角にいた。助けてくれたのはホームレスらしき不思議な老人、ウィリー。彼は廃墟と化したその通りを「ゴースト・アベニュー」と呼び、つぶれた映画館の跡へとエドを導く。そこで町の人にも忘れられ、まさしく「ゴースト」のような生活を送るホームレスの一団と出会ったエドは、自分が知らなかった世界の一面を目の当たりにする。
　店も財産も失ってやけになるエドに、ウィリーは「君はパイ職人だが、本当のパイが何でできているかを知らない」と語った。かつてパイ焼きの名人だった亡き母に言われた言葉とも重なり、エドは長い夜を泣き明かす。
　「パイは甘くなることも、すっぱくなってしまうこともあるけど、大事な人と一緒に食べれば、いつだっておいしいのよ」

Professor Willy

朝がやってきた時、エドは廃棄されたドラム缶とあり合わせの材料を使って、ウィリーたちに質素なパイを焼いた。決して立派なものではないが、心のこもったパイ——エドがはじめて誇りを持てる自分だけのパイだった。そのパイを口にして幸せそうに微笑むウィリーたちを見て、エドは今までの自分に足りなかったものがなんだったかを悟った。

　行方不明だった猫も無事に戻り、新しい一歩を踏み出したかに見えたエド。しかし、町の再開発計画はゴースト・アベニューにも迫っていて、再び否応なく運命の渦へ巻き込まれていくことを、エドはまだ知らなかった……。(『ビッグ・ファット・キャットとゴースト・アベニュー』)

The "Ghosts"

You know this town...

BFC BOOKS SERIES / PART 4 (season 2)

You know this street...

And you know this man.

But some things have changed since the last time you saw him.
It has been a long month for Ed Wishbone.

"George! Cherry! We need more cherry!" Ed shouted as he handed the last slice of cherry pie to a customer.

George was pulling a freshly baked banana chocolate pie out of the barrel^(ドラム缶) oven. He shouted to Ed.

"Gotcha!^(Got you)"

George handed the pie over to Paddy and started running down the street to the old cinema. They kept several extra^(予備の) pies there, just in case.

"W-where do you want this?" Paddy asked Ed.

"Below the counter somewhere," Ed told Paddy hurriedly as he turned back to a waiting customer.

"I'm sorry, ma'am. What can I get for you today?"

"I'll take a slice of that new lemon pie... and of course, two slices of blueberry, as usual."

"That'll be 75 cents."

"Are you sure? I feel like I'm cheating you. Paying you only 75 cents for such a wonderful pie."

"Thank you. But don't worry. We're doing fine."

"Well, God bless you. I hope you can do something about this long waiting line though."

"I'm sorry, ma'am. I'll try. Have a nice day."

"You too, now."

Ed ducked down under the counter for a moment and whispered to Paddy.

"I'm going to check the pies in the oven. Watch the shop for me, okay, Pad?"

"Uh... I-I'm not sure, Ed."

Paddy looked doubtful but Ed was already dashing out the side door.

Behind the trailer, there was a small outdoor kitchen. Ed and George had made three ovens out of barrels, steel panels, and pieces of wire. The smell of butter and sugar was everywhere.

Willy and the cat were playing around while Frank watched nearby, sitting in an old toy wagon. At least, Willy was playing. The cat's eyes were much more serious, focused on the pies in the oven.

Ed spoke to Willy as he opened the first oven and peeked inside.

"Will, please keep that cat out of the kitchen. It's not clean."

"Oh, c'mon Ed. He deserves a piece, too," Willy protested.

"That cat already ate two whole pies this morning!"

Ed pointed his finger at the cat. The cat paid no attention. BeeJees grunted. He was sitting nearby on an old tractor tire.

"That cat bit me when I tried to pet him."

"Bit you?!" George said.

He had returned from the theater with a cherry pie in his hands. He was still out of breath. He showed his free hand to BeeJees. There were four great big slashes on his forearm.

"Look at this, man. That cat *attacked* me when I was baking a blueberry pie! I was almost killed, man!"

"George, watch out!"

Ed shouted just in time for George to dodge the cat's jump from behind. The cat soared through the air, a few inches below the cherry pie in George's hand. The cat landed and turned back in a very angry motion. George looked at the cat and gulped.

"Oh-oh... He's gonna kill me now."

"George, RUN!" everybody yelled together.

George was already running, the cat right behind him in full speed. The two dashed through the kitchen and went running down Ghost Avenue as everybody laughed behind. Ed laughed too, holding a fresh-baked country cheesecake in his hand.

It had been a long month. A long month on Ghost Avenue.

It had all begun as a simple joke. George, who used to be a handyman, had made Ed a sign that said "Ed's Magic Pie Shop." The sign was a token of appreciation for the pies that Ed baked for the people in the cinema. Ed had hung it happily in front of the cinema without much thought.

But the other homeless residents of Ghost Avenue who had heard stories about free pie, saw the sign and came in to get some for themselves. Some of them even left a few dimes and nickels.

George soon found an old deserted trailer at the northern end of Ghost Avenue and had painted it with leftover paint. The trailer was just the right size to create a small kitchen space, so Ed moved his outdoor kitchen there.

As the days went by, more and more people started to come buy pies, and not all of them were homeless. A few curious passing cars started to stop by, and several kind women who lived nearby had come to buy a slice of pie in the spirit of charity. They returned for more when they found out the pies were actually good.

Now the cat was coming back down the street. The cat's whiskers were covered with something red. It pretty much suggested the fate of the cherry pie. George came around the corner after the cat, covered with the rest of the cherry pie. Ed smiled in spite of losing another pie. The others laughed in an uproar. They laughed so hard that Ed didn't realize Paddy was shouting.

"E-Ed!!"

Ed finally heard Paddy calling him on the third shout and waved a hand at him.

"Sorry, Pad. Be back in a minute!"

"N-No, Ed!! You need to come back, n-now!"

Ed's smile faded when he saw that the crowd in front of the shop had grown. Grown a lot. He stood there in awe, his heart beating faster and faster. He knew something had gone wrong.

Jeremy Lightfoot Jr. was afraid of his father.

He had always been afraid of him, even as a small child. He felt that his father was always disappointed with him, and therefore, always angry.

He never knew his mother. There was nobody to protect him from his father when he was a child. So he tried desperately to be a good son. He tried and tried, but nevertheless his father was always angry.

Now, as he stood at the door to his father's study, his hands were shaking. Jeremy would be thirty-one years old this year, but he still felt like a ten-year-old boy.

Jeremy's cat, Mr. Jones, appeared out of nowhere and brushed his tail on Jeremy's foot. Jeremy petted Mr. Jones with a slightly trembling hand. It made him feel a little better.

"You wait for me here, okay?"

Mr. Jones purred. Jeremy straightened his collar and tie and took a deep breath. He grabbed the doorknob and after one last moment of hesitation, turned it.

"Sir. You asked me to..." Jeremy said in a shaking voice as he stepped inside.

"Shut the door, you moron."

His father's cold voice filled the room.

Jeremy closed the door and stood nervously beside it. His father was watching the morning news on television and didn't even look back. The new bodyguard, Billy Bob, was standing at the far wall.

Jeremy didn't know why his father had hired Billy Bob. He already had two-dozen bodyguards around the house. But his father had told him Billy Bob was different.

And he was. Jeremy had felt it since the first time he had seen the man. There was a true coldness in the way Billy Bob moved. And he almost never talked.

"How is your business?" Jeremy's father asked suddenly. Jeremy was surprised. His father almost never asked him anything. Feeling a sense of relief, Jeremy took a step forward.

"Great, sir. Zombie Pies is really taking off. You should see the numbers. We're the fastest growing chain in the whole..."

"Good. Close it down."

Jeremy stopped on his first step, stunned in shock.

"Uh... excuse me?"

"I said, close down the pie shops. I need the space to promote the rehabilitation project."

Jeremy just stood there, forgetting even to breathe.

"Did you, or did you not, hear me?" his father demanded, still not moving his eyes from the television screen.

"I... I can't do that, sir. Even if it's your order. It's my shop." Jeremy's voice grew smaller and smaller. "The kids love my shops. They really love Zombie Pies."

    Jeremy's father said nothing. He was watching the television screen in silence. The morning news was showing the top news — something about a government scandal in Washington.

    "Please let me keep the shops. I really need this."

    "Your so-called shops will last for maybe another six months," Jeremy Lightfoot Sr. said finally. He spoke in a harsh, cold tone.

    "Then they'll get tired of your pies and your shops will be forgotten."

    "I'll try harder! I'll make it work! Please give me a chance to..."

    "Quiet."

    "Father..." Jeremy protested.

    "I said, shut up!" Jeremy's father suddenly raised his voice. He leaned forward for a closer look at the television screen. "Billy Bob, turn up the sound."

    Billy Bob took out the remote control and pushed the volume switch. The voice of a reporter boomed out of the speaker, filling the quiet room with a sudden burst of excitement.

"...As you can see, a small miracle has happened here on the deserted northwest side of Everville. People are returning to this once well-known shopping district. A twenty-nine-year-old man, Ed Wishbone, has started a small pie shop in the ruins of an old trailer. This is his kitchen. He says that all of his utensils are fully sanitized and everything is safe and clean. Let's ask Mr. Wishbone himself about his pies."

The camera moved through the side door of the pie shop and captured a shot of Ed, all red with embarrassment to the rims of his ears. Though his father didn't notice, Jeremy opened his eyes wide when he saw Ed on the screen.

"Do you really make these pies in that backyard? They're really good. Sweet... but not too sweet."

"Uh... thank you."

"Are you thinking of entering the state pie festival this weekend?"

"Pie festival?"

"The Annual State Pie Festival is held this year at the Everville Mall. You should consider entering. The prize this year is twenty thousand dollars!"

"I... I don't know. I really..."

Ed was cut off by the loud applause of the customers outside.

"I think your customers know."

The reporter smiled and gave Ed a wink.

"So now you've seen it, one man's journey(旅路) to save the old streets of Everville. And from the way people are gathering(集まる), who knows? He just might succeed(成功する). This is Glen Hamperton reporting from Ever..."

Billy Bob turned the television off. Jeremy Senior had raised his hand in the air.

"This is bad," Jeremy's father said to Billy Bob. "We can't afford having this man become any more popular than he is now."

"Yes sir," Billy Bob replied.

"As for this pie festival..." Jeremy Senior turned his armchair once more towards his son, took a deep breath, and spoke. "You might as well have that chance of yours. Stop this man from winning the contest and perhaps I will reconsider the termination of your enterprise."

"Will... will you really..."

"Do you, or do you not, want a chance?"

"Yes, sir. I'll try my best."

"Your best is far from enough. Try harder."

That said, Jeremy Senior simply turned away towards Billy Bob. "Billy Bob, come here."

With that, his father seemed to have forgotten he was there. He could probably stand there for an hour, but his father would never notice him. Jeremy Jr. stepped silently out of the room. Only Mr. Jones was waiting for him there, sitting quietly in the middle of the long, empty hallway. Mr. Jones purred.

"It's okay," Jeremy said in a sad voice. "I'm used to it. Nothing new."

Jeremy picked the cat up and held it close. Its warmth was comforting in the lifeless coldness of his father's house. The floor of the corridor was covered with the most expensive carpet on the market and the ceiling was decorated with golden ornaments.

Jeremy had lived in this huge mansion for his entire life, but had always felt lost in the seemingly endless corridors of the place. It looked so much like his life.

Fabulous, but empty.

"Now, *that* is something you don't see everyday," Ed said to George.

He was staring with widened eyes out of the side door of the Magic Pie Shop. George poked his head out from behind Ed and saw it too.

"Damned if I'm seeing that," George muttered, nearly dropping the apple he was peeling.

The cat was eating a piece of piecrust directly from Frank's hand. If Ed, George, or anybody else tried that, the result would be one less hand.

"Frank's good with animals, that's for sure," George said, shaking his head with disbelief.

"That's not an animal. That's a beast," Ed said, staring at the cat. It glared back at him.

The sunset signaled the end of another day for the Magic Pie Shop. Newly baked pies were lined on the table, ready for tomorrow. They gave off the sweet, spicy smell of hot cinnamon.

Hordes of people who had seen the news came rushing in for pies immediately after the broadcast. Ed sold every single slice of pie in the shop before closing for the day.

"Yo, Ed. Apples done, man. What next?"

George tossed the last peeled apple into the water bucket and washed his hands.

"Wow. You're getting faster everyday. Well... maybe you can help Willy and Pad clean the ovens."

"Sure thing," George said and went out the back door.

The sun was almost down. Orange rays came through the doorway. Ed whistled a tune as he knelt down below the counter to get a new bowl.

"Wishbone."

Ed froze as he got up. He found himself face to face with Jeremy Lightfoot Jr. He also noticed the big shadow standing behind him.

"I'm afraid we're closed," Ed replied, almost a whisper.

George and the others were in the backyard kitchen. He was alone in the shop. Jeremy tossed a flier on top of the counter.

"Take it. It's the entry form for this weekend's pie contest."

Ed remained motionless.

"Take it, Wishbone!" Jeremy said abruptly. This made Ed grab the flier. "You think you're so good. Come prove it."

"I don't want to be in a contest," Ed protested to Jeremy. "This shop is all I want. Please leave us alone."

Jeremy made a face of disgust.

"You lying coward," he said. "You would love to win, but you're afraid you'll lose. I bet you've never fought for anything in your whole life."

Ed kept his eyes on Billy Bob. But Jeremy's words echoed in his ear.

"Wishbone! Stop ignoring me!"

Jeremy's voice rose even higher in anger. He didn't know why he was getting so mad at this man he hardly knew. He didn't even know why he had come here.

"Shop! You call this dump a shop!? A Magic Pie Shop, huh? What does *magic* mean anyway!? Do you disappear or something?"

Jeremy snatched the sign of the Magic Pie Shop. He threw it on the ground and stepped on it.

"You need to..."

Jeremy never finished his sentence. Ed had suddenly grabbed him by the shoulder. Jeremy was caught by surprise. The man in front of him had suddenly become angry. Jeremy noticed this but couldn't understand why. He kept his foot on the sign.

"What are you..."

"Take your foot off my shop!" Ed said in a surprisingly strong voice.

"It's just a sign..."

Jeremy was cut off again.

"I said, take it off!"

Ed shoved Jeremy off the sign. Jeremy lost balance and fell down on his back.

Billy Bob's large hands grabbed Ed, pulled him over the counter and threw him to the ground. Ed scrambled over to the sign on the ground and covered it with the only thing he had. His body.

Billy Bob was instantly above him, kicking him on the side of his chest. It hurt badly and Ed couldn't stop coughing. Dust was flying all around him.

"Hey... you don't need to..."

Jeremy said to Billy Bob, but couldn't finish. He had seen the cold, hard look on Billy Bob's face. Billy Bob kicked Ed a second time. Ed coughed in pain again, but refused to get up. He gritted his teeth together to stop coughing and looked straight up at Jeremy. He tasted blood in his mouth, but was no longer scared.

"You're just like me," Ed said.

Billy Bob kicked him again.

"What?" Jeremy cried out. "Are you out of your mind!? I'm exactly not like you! I'm rich, I'm smart, I'm... rich, I'm..."

"You don't know what a pie is made of."

Jeremy tried hard to laugh but did not succeed. He shouted desperately at Billy Bob.

"This man is out of his mind. You kicked him too much!"

Ed smiled. This angered Jeremy even more. He cried out.

"What do you know!? What the fuck do you know!?"
（強調）

Billy Bob raised his foot over Ed's head. Ed squeezed his
ギュッとしぼる
eyes shut. But before Billy Bob could bring his foot down, a flash of red flew through the air. Billy Bob took a step back. Jeremy let out a cry of surprise at the same time.

"What..."

Ed opened his eyes and looked up.

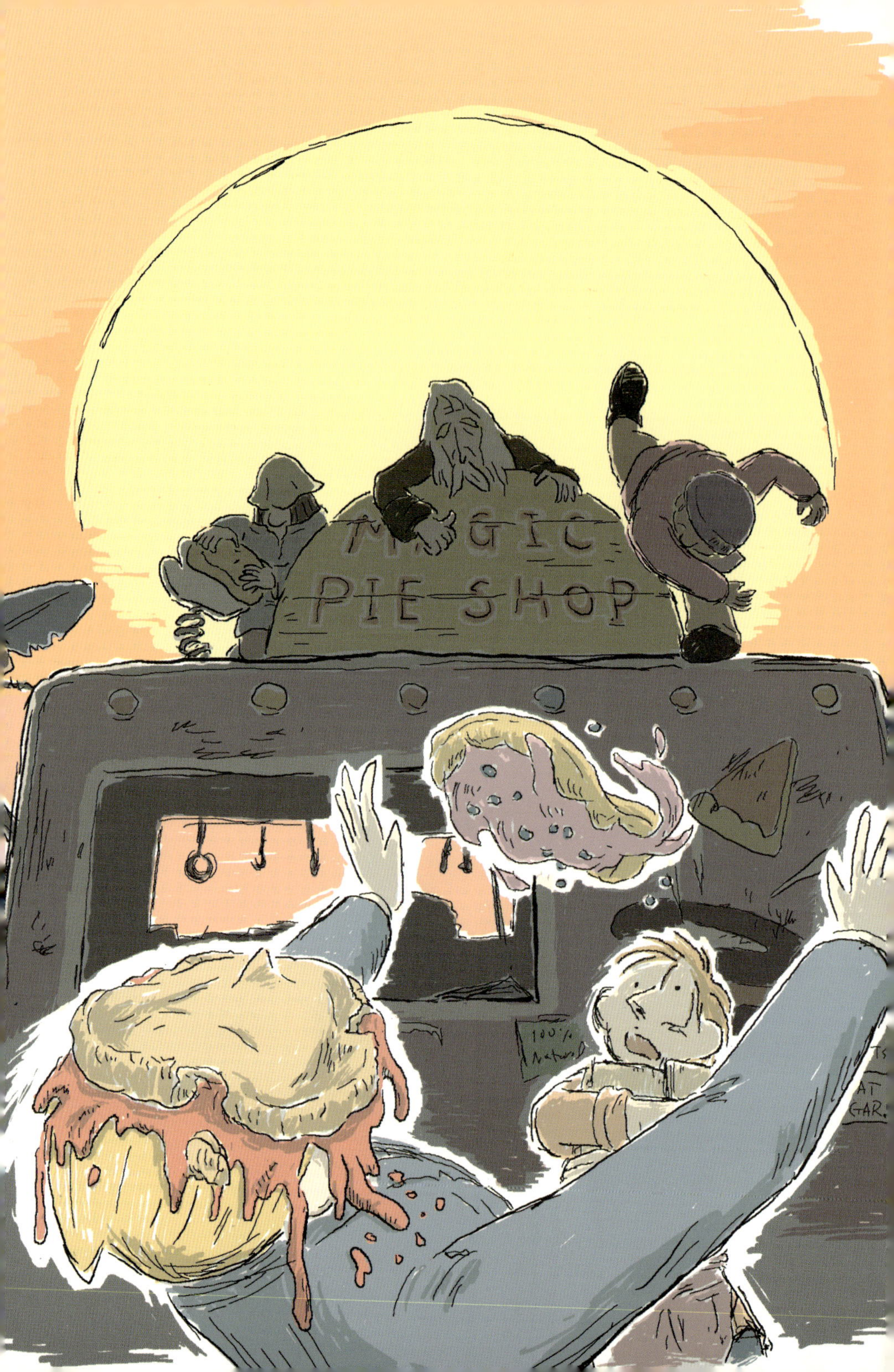
MAGIC
PIE SHOP
100% Natural

Pies were flying through the air!

Jeremy frantically wiped hot pie from his face, but as he was doing this, some got in his mouth. He stopped in silence. Several pies hit him but he didn't seem to notice. He just looked straight at Ed.

Billy Bob had mopped the pie off of his chest and was coming back at Ed. But this time, Jeremy shot his hand out in front of Billy Bob and stopped him.

"That's enough," Jeremy said to Billy Bob.

Jeremy and Ed looked at each other one last time. The pies had also stopped (probably out of ammunition).

"See you at the contest," Jeremy said.

Jeremy straightened his tie and walked off silently. Billy Bob, after a moment of hesitation, followed.

When Jeremy and Billy Bob were clearly out of sight(視界), George slid down from the roof and ran over to Ed.

"Ed! Man! You all right?"

Ed stood up. In his hands, he held the sign George had painted for him. It was broken in half.

"George... I'm sorry."

"Hey man, it's just a sign. I'll paint you another one tomorrow."

George laughed as if nothing had happened. It was such a light-hearted(軽快な) laugh that Ed smiled a little too.

"Magic ain't (is not) in the sign, man. Cheer up(元気を出す)! We won!"

With that, Paddy and Willy let out a great big cheer(歓声) of victory from the roof of the trailer. George patted Ed on the back. Ed gradually(次第に) began to laugh out loud too.

Everyone was laughing except for the cat. It just happened to come around the shop at that moment and was confronting(出くわす) the most shocking scene of its life.

Midnight.

A few hours later, the "ghosts" of Ghost Avenue were safely gathered around the fire inside the cinema. Ed had pretty much recovered and was now mixing ingredients for his new pie.

Everybody watched with curiosity as Ed took out a jar of pickles. A look of doubt crossed their faces as Ed minced the pickles and threw them into the bowl. But they managed to remain quiet while Ed added ingredients such as boiled eggs, grated cheese, and spinach. When Ed reached for the small yellow bottle, however, Willy finally spoke out.

"Ed! That's mustard," Willy cried as Ed poured mustard from the bottle into the bowl. Ed heard, but continued to pour the yellow liquid until he had mixed the last drop into the recipe. Everybody watched with sour faces. Ed looked around the table, saw the faces, and said with a smile, "It's okay. It's my new pie."

"Ed. That's mustard," Willy repeated simply.

"Of course, it's mustard. It's a mustard pie."

This caused everybody to grimace.

"It's not that bad," Ed quickly added.

Everyone replied with groans and deep sighs. Ed, a little frustrated, took a freshly baked pie from under the table and placed it in front of everybody.

"Here. I baked one earlier today. Have a taste."

Everyone took a step back from the table. A faint smell of mustard was mixed with the crisp smell of piecrust.

"Go ahead. Have a taste," Ed insisted.

The men looked at each other hopefully, but no one volunteered. Reluctantly, they played a game of scissors-paper-stone to decide. Willy lost. Willy turned towards the pie with a sad look and found Ed twitching his eyebrows at him. He smiled quickly.

"Uh, Ed. I'm happy to have the honor of participating in this... this science experiment."

"It's not an experiment," Ed said.

"Oh, I'm sure that my sacrifice will someday be useful to the further development of mankind. Well, so long everybody."

Willy waved his hand and picked up a piece of the mustard pie. He raised it to his nose and smelled it. Everyone held their breath. After a moment, Willy collapsed to the floor. The others burst out laughing.

"The smell!? Just with the smell!? No way!!" Ed shouted.

By this time, George, Paddy and Frank were all laughing so hard that they could hardly keep standing.

"I'm telling you! It's not that bad!"

Ed was angry and the others were busy laughing. No one except BeeJees realized that Willy had fallen down awkwardly. BeeJees leaned over the table to whisper to Willy, who was still lying on the floor.

"Hey, Willy. You can get up now. We got your point. Willy?"

BeeJees's face turned white when he saw that Willy was lying face down.

"No! It's not the pie! It's his heart! It's doing it again!"

BeeJees jumped across the table to Willy. The others were still laughing.

"What?" Ed asked.

He could not hear what BeeJees had said because of the laugher. But everyone stopped laughing when BeeJees held up Willy's limp body.

"Prof! C'mon! Prof!"

Ed froze. He couldn't understand what was happening. He cried out in almost sheer panic.

"BeeJees! What the hell is going on!?"

"Don't worry. It's not your pie," BeeJees turned back and replied quickly. Sweat was running down his forehead. "Willy's heart is in a real bad condition."

All Ed could say was, "Why isn't he in a hospital?"

"Because hospitals cost money."

"Use mine."

Ed took his wallet out instantly and held it out to BeeJees. A cold feeling was rising up in his heart. Willy wasn't moving. His mouth was half open, as if he had stopped breathing.

Grasping the situation at last, George and Paddy rushed over to Willy and started slapping his face. The night suddenly seemed a lot darker and colder.

"Hospital costs lots of money. At least two grand a week. And that's without any treatment," BeeJees said to Ed as he was giving CPR to Willy.

"He's not responding!" Paddy cried out, almost in tears.

"Oh no... This is bad, man. This is really bad."

George was sweating hard too. This was the first time Ed had seen George with a serious face. But Ed still couldn't move. All he could do was stand there and ask in a dumbfounded voice, "Isn't there a phone somewhere? We need an ambulance."

"You know there isn't a single working phone on this street," BeeJees said to Ed. He was angry. Probably not angry at Ed, but angry.

Beejees took a deep breath, trying to calm down.

"Besides..., no ambulance would come here at this time of night."

"Then what are we supposed to do? He's dying, isn't he?"

"Pray," BeeJees answered.

BeeJees, George, and Paddy were trying to do everything they could. But anybody could see this wasn't enough. Ed looked desperately around the theater and found a rusty shopping cart by the wall. He grabbed the cart and a few old blankets and hurried over to Willy.

"We have to get him to a hospital."

Ed reached for Willy's hand but BeeJees slapped his arm away. "Don't!"

"Why not!? For heaven's sake!"

"He wanted to die, Wishbone. If he's going to die, let him die here."

"That's insane!"

"Wishbone. You're just making this harder. Let him go."

Ed reached for Willy again. BeeJees started to stop him, but this time, Ed pushed him away and said to George, "C'mon and help me. We have to get him to a hospital."

George nodded and started helping Ed wrap Willy in one of the blankets. Together, they carried Willy over to the shopping cart. BeeJees just sat there on the ground shaking his head.

"I'm telling you, Wishbone. You're just increasing everyone's pain."

Ed finished tucking Willy into the blanket and turned back to BeeJees. He was scared. Part of him knew that BeeJees was probably right. But another part of him, the warmer, stronger part of him spoke.

"I know I'm naive. I just don't want to give up. I've given up too many things already."

The shopping cart flew through the theater doors, Ed and George pushing it from behind.

BeeJees watched the doors swing from the force of the passing shopping cart. He knew what was going to happen. He slumped to the ground, biting his lower lip as the tears came, one by one, down his dry cheek.

"Damn it, Wishbone. Why can't you understand? It's too late. We're all too late."

The night outside was cold and quiet. The moon was almost full, with a perfect sky behind it — no clouds at all. There was no one in sight. A car passed every once in a while, but other than that, everything was silent except for the rattle of their shopping cart.

Ed and George pushed the cart down Ghost Avenue until they came to the intersection of Lake Every Drive. They crossed the intersection carefully and continued walking south. The hospital was about a mile further down the road. It had been easy until then. But when they entered the downtown district, the road changed uphill.

It was not a steep incline. Perhaps you wouldn't notice it if you were walking. But it made a pretty big difference if you were a child or a jogger — or even two men pushing a shopping cart.

The rattle of the rusted cart suddenly broke off when one of the front wheels snapped free. The cart was forced to a stop. Ed knelt down and examined the broken wheel.

George came over to Ed and whispered to him, "No way we can repair this."

George was right. A sense of unease filled Ed as he said, "I guess we'll have to carry the cart."

"Maybe I can carry Willy on my back," George suggested.

"It... might not be a good idea to rock him too much. Besides we still have a mile to go. Can you take the front end? I'll get the back."

"No problem."

George nodded.

And so they went. Two shadows in the moonlight carrying a man in a shopping cart. Sweat rolled down Ed's face, although the first hundred steps were not hard.

But after ten minutes, the weight of the cart started to feel like the weight of a small car. Ed's arms and feet were getting weaker and weaker by the moment.

Ed glanced back over his shoulder. He shouldn't have. Fear ran through him as he realized that they still had more than half way to go. The hospital was a small red glow at the top of the hill. It wasn't that far, but it seemed miles away.

The only thing that kept Ed moving was Willy's lifeless face lying within the pile of musty blankets.

He had to keep walking. He had to.

Son. You are a baker.

Professor Willy was the first person who had ever called him a baker. He would never forget that. He would never, ever forget that.

One at a time, he took careful steps forward. His legs were weak now. One wrong step and he might lose balance.

As they passed the elementary school, Ed thought he heard someone say something in a really soft voice. He thought that maybe George was saying something to encourage himself. But it wasn't George. He could see that, even from behind.

Then who —

"Willy?" Ed said.

George stopped and looked back. Willy's mouth was moving slightly. Ed leaned forward and listened carefully. At first, he thought Willy was just breathing. But then he was able to hear the soft sounds coming from Willy's mouth.

"He's... singing," Ed said to George with an amazed look.

"Singing?" George gasped and listened. "Oh, yeah. I hear it too."

It was such a soft and tender voice.

Ed and George started to walk again, but somehow it was easier this time. The hospital seemed closer and the cart seemed lighter. Ed noticed the full moon in the sky for the first time. And in spite of all the chaos, it was still beautiful.

A comfortable breeze circled around them. George began to sing along with Willy. It was a song Ed had heard millions of times, but he had never realized how beautiful it was until now.

Tears formed in his eyes. There were so many things he still had to learn. The world was so huge and so full of surprises.

The world is not a mustard pie, Ed.

No, it wasn't.

Ed closed his eyes and listened to Willy and George singing. And after a moment, he too, joined the song.

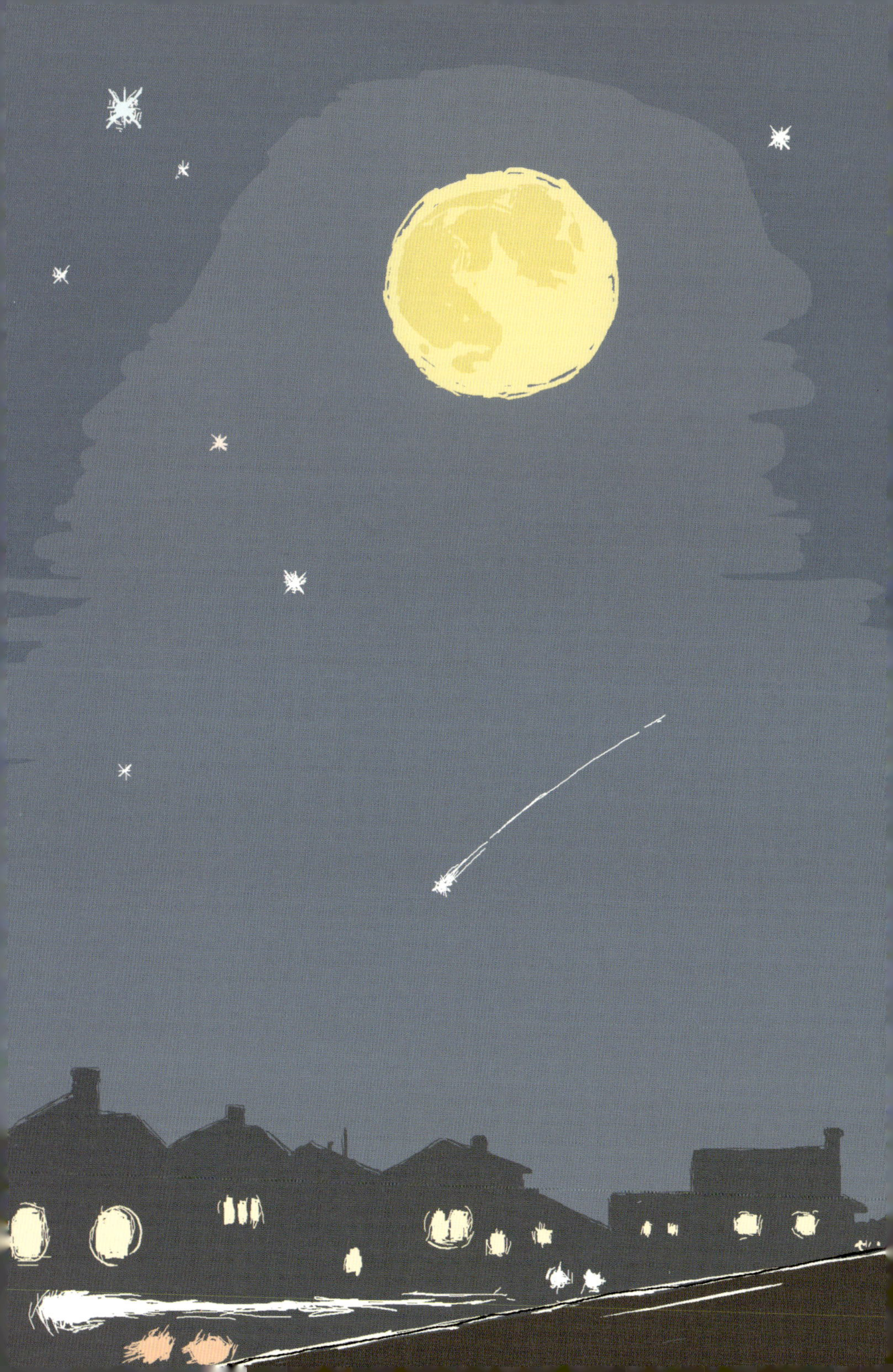

I see trees of green, red roses too
I watch them bloom for me and you
　　　　　　花咲く
And I think to myself
What a wonderful world

I see skies of blue, clouds of white
The bright blessed day and the dark sacred night
　　　　　祝福された　　　　　　　　聖なる
And I think to myself
What a wonderful world

I hear babies cry, I watch them grow
They'll learn much more than I'll ever know
And I think to myself
What a wonderful world
Yes I think to myself
What a wonderful world

Door.

Emergency.
緊急

Get help.

These were the only thoughts left in Ed's head when they finally reached the emergency entrance of the Everville Hospital. He somehow found some final dregs of strength in his legs and wobbled up to the doors.
残りカス　　　　　　　　　　　　　力
よろよろ歩く

They were locked. Ed banged his fist on the doors.
ドンドンたたく　こぶし

"Someone! Someone, help us! We need help!"

The lights were dark inside. Nobody answered Ed's call.

Ed took a quick look at the shopping cart. Willy had stopped singing and was as quiet as before. George was totally exhausted and was down on his hands and knees. Ed wanted to give up and lie down too, but he continued to hit the door.
疲れ切った

Then suddenly, the sound of a window opening came from above.

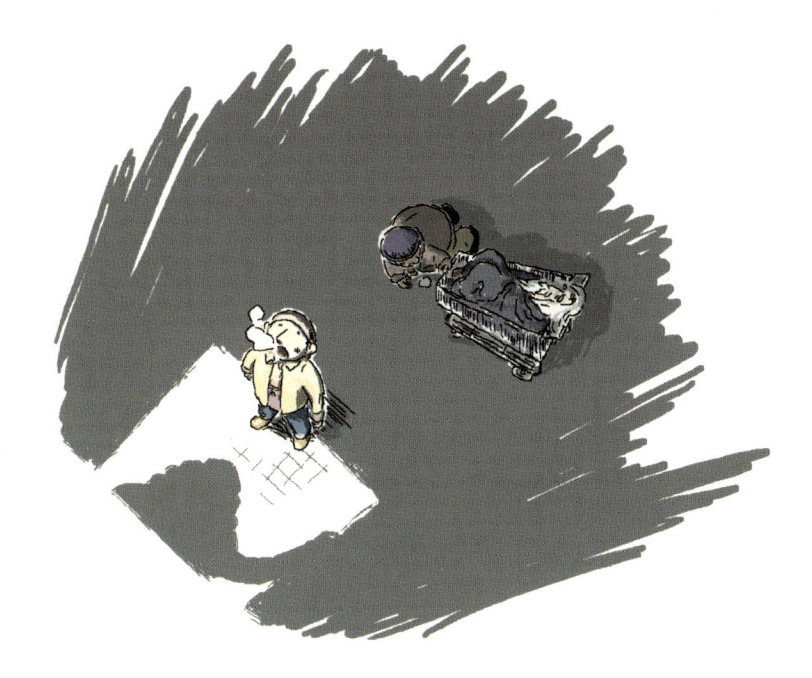

Ed backed away a few steps and found a nurse looking down at them suspiciously.

"Ma'am, we need help," Ed said.

The nurse didn't answer, but her eyes studied Ed and the others carefully — their dirty, ripped clothing, Willy's long beard, and the rusted old shopping cart.

"Please. We need a doctor. If it's money, I have some. And I promise I'll get more in a few days."

The nurse started to close the windows.

"No! Please! We really need help! Here!" Ed shouted desperately as he emptied his wallet on the sidewalk. He scattered small change and a few dollar bills around him. "This is all the money I have now, but...!!"

The window closed shut with a cold sound. Ed was left in the dark with only silence for an answer.

"Please... we..."

Ed's voice faded as he slumped down on the ground.

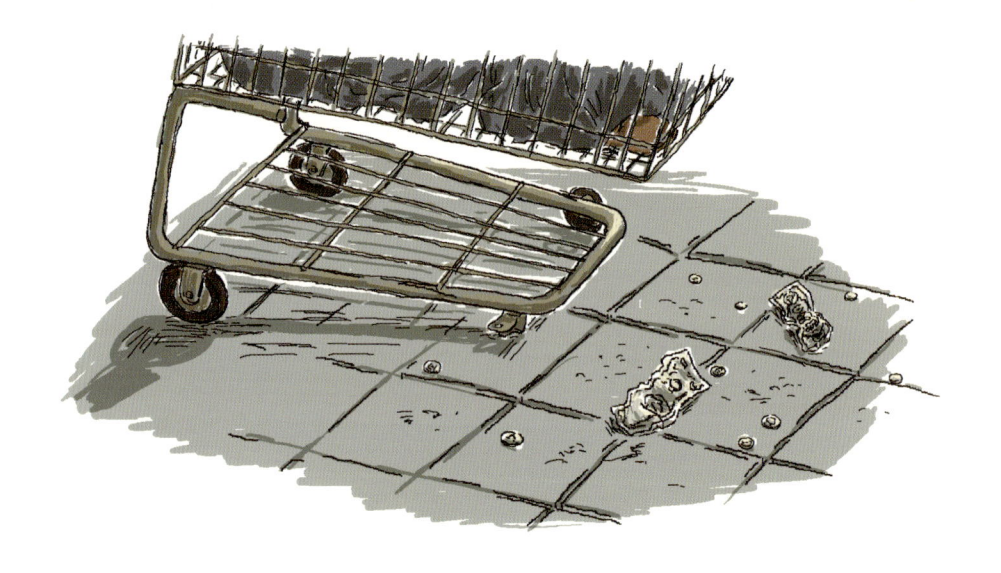

George crawled over to Ed and put his hands on Ed's shoulders. Looking at George's face, Ed realized that George had known this would happen. But he had helped him anyway.

"At least we tried, man."

George smiled. It was a true smile.

"I bet the Prof's happy too. Yo, man. Maybe it's time to give up. Leave things to good old Jesus upstairs."

Ed sat still on the concrete. He knew George was right. Just as BeeJees had been right all along.

Ed gripped his thighs and lowered his head close to the ground. He felt hope running out of him. He knew he was about to give up.

Ed had almost never prayed in his life, but at that moment, he prayed from the bottom of his heart. He prayed for courage. The courage not to give up.

"Yo, c'mon Ed," George called.

As Ed was getting up, something fell out of his chest pocket. It floated in the air for a moment, then landed silently on the ground. Ed picked it up.

"Yo. Let's go home. I think Willy's just sleeping. He'll be fine until tomorrow morning."

George caught Ed under the arm and helped him to his feet. Ed was still holding the flier. His eyes were glued to the words printed on it.

As he read those words, something Willy had said to him a while before circled around his mind.

Ed. Willy had said. *You are a baker.*

You are a baker.

You are a baker.

TO BE CONTINUED

Big Fat Cat
AND
THE MAGIC SHOP PIE

をもっと読み込む

セリフについて、少し

『ビッグ・ファット・キャットとマジック・パイ・ショップ』いかがだったでしょうか。今回はセリフがたくさん登場するので、くだけた表現に手こずったという方も多いかもしれません。前回の『ビッグ・ファット・キャットとゴースト・アベニュー』では「とばす」という技術に的を絞って解説をしましたが、今回もやはり難しいところがあれば、「とばす」ことはどんどん活用してください。面白くなければ読書とは言えません。分からなくてイライラするより、気持ちよくとばしてしまった方が物語を楽しめます。

しかし、セリフは作品の中心部分です。さすがにとばすのは不安になるかもしれません。その上、通常の英文と比べると格段に読みにくいものです。分かったような、分からないような感じがして、釈然としない場合も多いと思います。

これにははっきりとした原因があります。それさえ分かれば、ややこしいセリフも怖くはありません。そもそもセリフはなんでややこしくなるのか――まずはそこから考えてみましょう。

「決まり文句」という呪文

もともと話し言葉は書き言葉とちがって、言い直したり、編集したりできないので、簡単な文しか使うことができません。それなのに英語のセリフを読んでいると、まったく意味不明の文やフレーズに突き当たることがあります。これを辞書で引いてみると、ものすごく難解な言葉だったり、パズルのようにややこしい内容だったりします。そんな時には「英語って本当に難しい」と感じて、途方に暮れてしまうかもしれません。

でも、本当にそうなのでしょうか？

本当にみんな、日常的にそんな難しいことを考えて、英語を話しているのでしょうか？

日本語で考えてみてください。——何かひどいことをされた時のセリフに、古い言い回しですが、「そんな殺生な！」というのがあります。これを外国人が聞いたとしましょう。当然「殺生」などという言葉は聞いたこともありませんから、アメリカ版の和英辞書を取り出して調べてみるはずです。すると、こんな意味に当たります。「殺生：生きるものを殺すこと」。これではちんぷんかんぷんです。おそらく日本人の精神の中には仏教の心が根づいていて、外国人には分からない感覚があるのだろうと考えるのではないでしょうか。

とんでもない話です。

おそらく現代で「そんな殺生な！」という表現を使うのは、冗談めかしてオーバーに何かを言っている時だけです。その時にとっさにこの言葉が口から出てきたとしたら、それには次の三つの理由があるはずです。

1. 誰かが言っているのを聞いて、面白いと思ったことがある。
2. 自分の性格に合った言い方だと考えている。
3. 今までも似たようなシチュエーションでそう言ってきた。

どれを取っても、言っている本人ですら意味が分かっていない可能性が高いはずです。誰かがその言葉を使っているのを聞いて、同じ場面になった時に自分もなんとなく使っている言葉——これが「決まり文句」というやつです。日本語も英語もこの決まり文句であふれています。

「決まり文句」にルールはあてはまりません。いわば呪文のようなもので、この言葉を唱えれば、こういうことを相手が感じるという固定されたフレーズです。いつも同じ効果があるので覚えてしまうと便利ですが、知らなければ意味が分からなくても当然です。

上のイラストを見て、「このフキダシに適切なセリフを入れてください」とアメリカ人に頼むと、返ってくる答えは何種類かに限定されるはずです。現実でも、同じような状況に遭遇すれば、同じような反応が返ってくるでしょう。この場面でとっさに使われる「決まり文句」というのが確実にあるからです。

会話とモールス信号の共通点

　日本語でも英語でも、会話はごく簡単な文の間に、たまに「決まり文句」が入ってできています。構成としてはモールス信号によく似ているかもしれません。ツーツー、という何でもない文が続いて、トンとリズムをとるような感じで決まり文句が入ります。

　こんな感じで会話は進みます。実際の文にこれをあてはめると、次に登場する例のように、青にぬった「普通の文」の間に、オレンジ色の「決まり文句」がリズムよく入るのが分かります。

Jeremy Lightfoot Jr.'s
NOT A BAD LIFE

Big Fat Cat and the Magic Pie Shop

Hi! How are you? I saw that new horror movie "Big Fat Cat" yesterday. It was horrible. Bad as can be. I hope they never make a sequel. Well, see you later!

　会話は言語の中でも特殊な分野です。勉強というより、純粋に慣れです。「ああ、こういう時はそう言うのか」「あ、でもこっちのセリフの方が自分らしいな」「そうか、ああ反応すれば効果的だ」そういった経験の繰り返しで、会話は成り立っています。簡単な文の上に、少しパンチの効いた「決まり文句」を入れていく——それが「しゃべる」ということです。また、「決まり文句」を言っている間は頭の中を休めることができるので、その隙に次に話すことを考える余裕も出てきます。

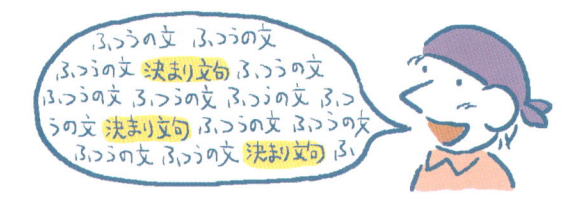

BFC流英会話教室へようこそ

　小説のセリフの中でも「うわ、難しい！」と思うものに出会ったら、たいていそれは「決まり文句」です。だから、一回目で読めなくても心配しないでください。今回、『ビッグ・ファット・キャットとマジック・パイ・ショップ』では今までのBFCシリーズよりも日常的で多彩な会話がたくさん出てきます。「決まり文句」や「スラング（俗語）」

Today was Halloween Day. Halloween was the best time of the year for Zombie Pies. This year, a lot of kids were ordering Zombie Pies for their Halloween party and sales were rocketing sky-high. Jeremy's new seasonal pie "Chamber of Horrors" was the top seller this month, and Jeremy couldn't be happier.

rocketing ＝ロケットのように飛ぶ

などもかなり登場しています。そのため、今回の解説では「決まり文句」にアンダーラインを引いて、詳しく説明してみました。
　いつものことですが、「決まり文句」をいちいち覚える必要はありません。たとえ覚えても、自分の性格と合っていないものなら一生使うことはありません。なんとなく読んで、面白いと思う決まり文句があれば、自然に頭に残ります。それが自分の使える「決まり文句」です。ほかのいらないものまで覚えようとするよりは、もう一度物語本編を読み返す方がずっと有意義です。
　日本の教室で「英会話」と呼ばれているものは、基本的にこの「決まり文句」をたくさん覚えることを指します。確かに「決まり文句」を覚えれば、多少のコミュニケーションはとれますが、どうしても限界が出てきます。また自分の性格にふさわしくないしゃべり方になってしまうこともあります。やはり遠回りでも自分の言葉を探して、ひとつひとつ自分に合った「決まり文句」を見つけていくしか本当の英語にたどり着く道はありません。
　誰がどんな決まり文句を使うのか――また、別のキャラクターが同じ決まり文句を使ったら、どう印象が変わるのか――それに今まで分からなかった声の大きさ、セリフの間、セリフの量などの要素を感じながら、もう一度『ビッグ・ファット・キャットとマジック・パイ・ショップ』を読んでみてください。
　次ページからは **BFC** 流の英会話教室へご招待しましょう！

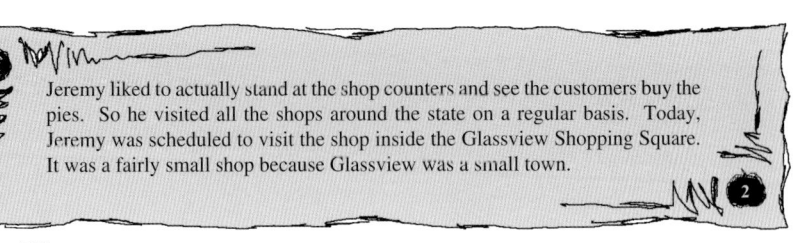

Jeremy liked to actually stand at the shop counters and see the customers buy the pies. So he visited all the shops around the state on a regular basis. Today, Jeremy was scheduled to visit the shop inside the Glassview Shopping Square. It was a fairly small shop because Glassview was a small town.

basis ＝周期

Big Fat Cat and the Magic Pie Shop

pp.12-13 / まずは手始めに

"George! Cherry! We need more cherry!"
Gotcha! ①

W-where do you want this?
Below the counter somewhere. ②

　まず最初にセリフが出てくるのは、本文の **12** ページです。
　開幕と同時に威勢よく指示を出しているエド——今までとは微妙に印象がちがいます。わずかな差ですが、しゃべり方も変わりました。決して横暴な口調ではないのですが、忙しいために最小限の言葉しか口にしていません。
　たとえば②のセリフなどは、今までのエドならもう少し丁寧に「**Please put it below the counter somewhere.**」というところですが、ここでのエドは省ける部分はすべて省いて話しています。ほかのところでも、エドのセリフは今回、短くなっていることが多いので気をつけてください。
　ジョージのセリフの「ガッチャ！」（①）は **Got you!** の省略形です。「あなたをつかんだ」が転じて「了解！」という意味になっていますが、通常の **yes** や **sure** 以上に「任せとけ」という自信とはりきりが隠されています。これが「決まり文句」です。ただ、これはかなり癖のある決まり文句なので、ジョージのようなお調子者でないと、なかなかうまく使えないかもしれません。

Zombie Pies Glassview Store was booming with business. The eat-in space was filled with people throughout the day, and several cars were always lining up at the drive-thru. Jeremy watched as the kids went home happily with their mothers, a "Chamber of Horrors" pie in their hands. ③

booming＝好況である

p.13 / カウンター越しに老婦人と会話を

Ed: I'm sorry, ma'am. What can I get for you today?

Old lady: I'll take a slice of that new lemon pie... and <u>of course</u>, two slices of blueberry, <u>as usual</u>.

Ed: That'll be 75 cents.

Old lady: <u>Are you sure?</u> I feel like I'm cheating you. Paying you only 75 cents for such a wonderful pie.

Ed: <u>Thank you</u>. But don't worry. We're doing fine.

Old lady: <u>Well</u>, <u>God bless you</u>. I hope you can do something about this long waiting line though. ①

② **Ed:** <u>I'm sorry, ma'am</u>. I'll try. <u>Have a nice day</u>.

Old lady: <u>You too</u>, <u>now</u>. ③

　13ページに入って、いよいよ「決まり文句」のオンパレードです。ファーストフードのお店などではマニュアルがあるように、店員と客の会話というのはほとんどが決まり文句で構成されています。仲間内に指示を出している前ページとちがって、ここでのエドは老婦人を相手に丁寧な接客調で話しています。そのため、言葉が省略されることもありません。

　老婦人の方もエド以上に決まり文句が目立ちます。年輩のキャラクターは特に決まり

Late in the evening, Jeremy noticed a young mother-like woman standing near the ice-cream stands. She had been standing there for nearly an hour, but she didn't seem to order anything. Jeremy also realized that she seemed very sad. And that was really strange, because no one was ever sad in Zombie Pies. ④

文句を使う傾向があり、逆に落ち着いた性格に見せようとするなら、ちょっと古めかしい決まり文句を多用すればいいとも言えます。

　老婦人の決まり文句のうち、特に注目したいのは **God bless you.** と **now** の二つです。**God bless you.**（①）はそのままとらえると「神があなたを祝福しますように」と、ひどく大げさに聞こえますが、キリスト教が日常にとけ込んでいるアメリカでは、「Thank you very much.」と大差のない言葉です。

　now（③）の方ですが、これは実に便利な言葉です。本来の意味は「今」という時間を表す言葉ですが、この会話のように、文章の前や後に付録として置かれていて、明らかに「今」を表していない場合には「さて」「いいわね」などのように、たいして意味のない「間」として働きます。以前登場した「**You know**」などとも似ているのですが、こちらはとてもおだやかな響きのある決まり文句です。会話に一拍おきたい時の必需品です。

　エドのセリフの最初の二つと、最後の **Have a nice day.**（②）はこういうカウンター越しの接客の時に使われる定番のセリフです。失言が許されない仕事の現場では、すべての動作や問いかけにある程度決まり文句を用意しておくのがふつうです。特にカウンターでは、お客さんをさばくスピードが売り上げにも関わるので、口に出す言葉をいちいち考えている暇はありません。エドもおそらく、こういったセリフをほかのお客さんにも繰り返しているはずです。

　会話は決まり文句の量が増えるほど、スムーズでプロらしい会話になります。楽に会話をしたいのならば、たくさん「決まり文句」のフレーズをためこんでおくと、とっさの時にも困りません。

　ただ、決まり文句は便利ですが、聞き慣れた言葉だけに、あまり深い気持ちは伝わりません。愛の告白やお詫びの言葉など、本当に大切なことは、たどたどしくても自分が作った言葉でしゃべらなければ伝わらないのも本当です。

Finally, Jeremy went over to the woman and asked her. "Ma'am, we don't mind that you aren't buying anything. Zombie Pies is a fun place to be. So you're always welcome. But why are you so sad?"
The woman replied.
"My son lives in that hospital across the street."

pp.14-18 / 単語のアップグレード　その1

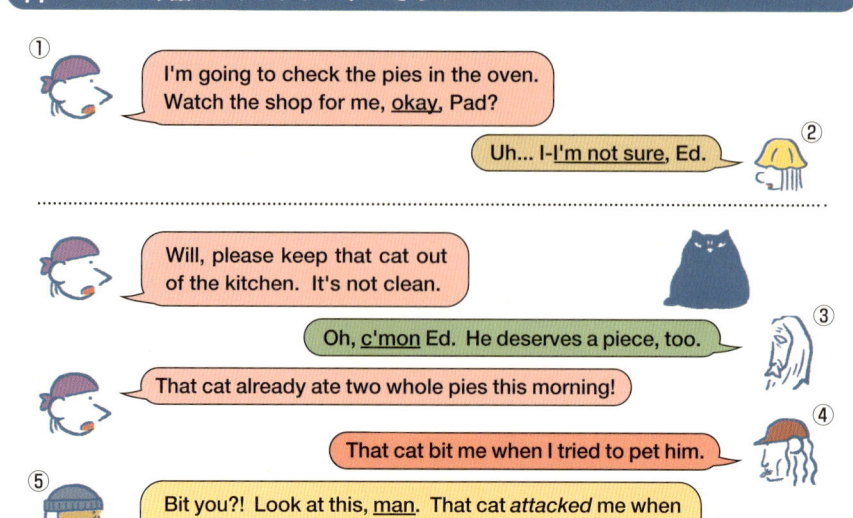

① I'm going to check the pies in the oven. Watch the shop for me, <u>okay</u>, Pad?

② Uh... I-<u>I'm not sure</u>, Ed.

Will, please keep that cat out of the kitchen. It's not clean.

③ Oh, <u>c'mon</u> Ed. He deserves a piece, too.

That cat already ate two whole pies this morning!

④ That cat bit me when I tried to pet him.

⑤ Bit you?! Look at this, <u>man</u>. That cat *attacked* me when I was baking a blueberry pie! I was almost killed, <u>man</u>!

　エドの **okay**（①）、パディの **I'm not sure.**（②）なども決まり文句ですが、ここで一番目立つものは、やはりウィリーの **c'mon**（③）です。**come on** を省略したもので、ふつうは「おいで」の意味を考えがちですが、「なあ、いいじゃないか」という感じの呼びかけとしても使えます。使い方としてはむしろこちらの方が多いかもしれません。自分の意見とちがう見解の人に「こっち側においでよ」という意味で呼びかけています。

　後半には英語独特の面白い要素が出てきます。それが「単語のアップグレード」です。ビージーズの「**bit**（かむ）された」（④）という愚痴に対して、ジョージがより大げさな「**attacked**（襲う）された」（⑤）という矢印で言い返しています。英語には同じような

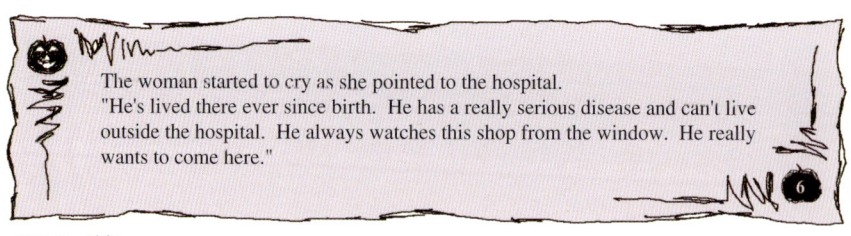

The woman started to cry as she pointed to the hospital.
"He's lived there ever since birth. He has a really serious disease and can't live outside the hospital. He always watches this shop from the window. He really wants to come here."

⑥

disease ＝病気

Big Fat Cat and the Magic Pie Shop

George, watch out!

Oh-oh... He's gonna kill me now.

George, RUN!

bite

E-Ed!!

Sorry, Pad.
Be back in a minute!

N-No, Ed!! You need to come back, n-now!

attack

kill

　意味でも、日常的なものから、ものすごく大げさなものまで、何段階かの強さの単語が用意されていることがよくあります。これらをうまく入れ替えて、この時のジョージのように矢印をより大げさなものに「アップグレード」することで、面白い会話を作ることができます。**bite → attack** と来て、矢印はついに **kill**（⑥）になってしまいます。よほど猫の攻撃が恐ろしかったのでしょう。

　頭につくはずの **I'll** が省略されていますが、**I'll be back in a minute.**（⑦）もよく使われる決まり文句です。「一分以内」と言っていますが、実際には「すぐに」ぐらいのイメージです。もっと短く、「**in a second**（一秒以内）」と表現することもあります。

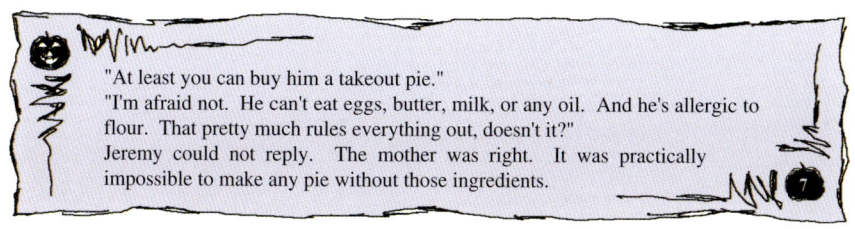

"At least you can buy him a takeout pie."
"I'm afraid not. He can't eat eggs, butter, milk, or any oil. And he's allergic to flour. That pretty much rules everything out, doesn't it?"
Jeremy could not reply. The mother was right. It was practically impossible to make any pie without those ingredients.

allergic＝アレルギー　rules＝規制する　practically＝事実上　ingredients＝原材料

pp.20-23 / ジェレミー親子の事情　その1

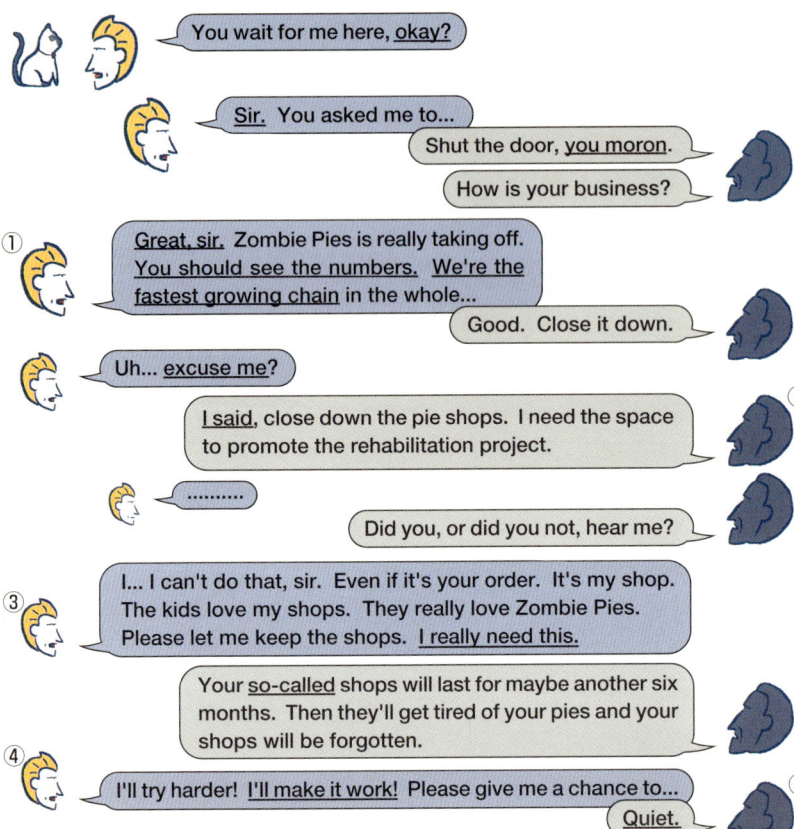

You wait for me here, okay?

Sir. You asked me to...

Shut the door, you moron.

How is your business?

① Great, sir. Zombie Pies is really taking off. You should see the numbers. We're the fastest growing chain in the whole...

Good. Close it down.

Uh... excuse me?

② I said, close down the pie shops. I need the space to promote the rehabilitation project.

....

Did you, or did you not, hear me?

③ I... I can't do that, sir. Even if it's your order. It's my shop. The kids love my shops. They really love Zombie Pies. Please let me keep the shops. I really need this.

Your so-called shops will last for maybe another six months. Then they'll get tired of your pies and your shops will be forgotten.

④ I'll try harder! I'll make it work! Please give me a chance to...

⑤ Quiet.

⑥ Father...

⑦ I said, shut up! Billy Bob, turn up the sound.

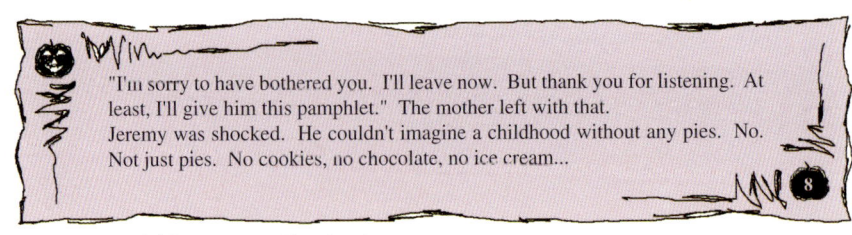

"I'm sorry to have bothered you. I'll leave now. But thank you for listening. At least, I'll give him this pamphlet." The mother left with that.
Jeremy was shocked. He couldn't imagine a childhood without any pies. No. Not just pies. No cookies, no chocolate, no ice cream... ⑧

bothered＝じゃまする　pamphlet＝パンフレット

ここでのジェレミー親子の会話は、会社の上司や軍隊の上官と部下がしゃべっているような印象です。父親のセリフはいっさいの反論を許さない強い口調で、矢印で始まる命令の文が多く含まれています。これに対してジェレミーの方は、sir をつけた敬語の形が多く、最後に一度だけ「父親」として呼びかけるところも（⑥）、よく用いられる「Dad」の形ではなく、とてもよそよそしい「Father...」という形です。しかも、それもあっさり父親の言葉に遮られてしまいます。

　You should see the numbers.（①）（数字を見てください）、We're the fastest growing chain（①）（もっとも成長の著しいチェーン店です）、I really need this.（③）（本当に必要なんです）、I'll make it work（④）（成功させてみせます／it は「ゾンビ・パイ」）などはすべて難しい文に見えますが、どれもこういう場面でよく用いられる決まり文句の一種です。逆にこういった表現はセリフの中でしか出てくることがありません。

　中盤や最後でのジェレミーの父親のように、I said-（②、⑦）と前置きして、自分が直前に言ったことを繰り返すのは、自分の言い分を相手に強制するための決まり文句です。

　また、決まり文句というなら、最後の方のジェレミーの父親のセリフ（⑦）は正にそうです。英語で「うるさい」と言う時の定番の言い方がこの shut up。「shut」は「ぴしゃっと閉じる」ことで、「口を閉じろ」と言っていることになります。その手前に出てくる「Quiet.」（⑤）というのは同じことをもう少し上品に言い換えた形で、学校の先生などが生徒を黙らせる時によく使っています。

　c'mon のような気軽な決まり文句がまったく出てこない親子の会話というのは、本当に冷たく悲しい響きがあります。ジェレミーはどんな思いでこの父親の言葉を聞いていたのでしょうか？

That night, Jeremy went home to his laboratory and looked through all his recipes. But it was apparent that pies were impossible to make without at least some sort of oil. Jeremy tried to give up many times, but his mind kept reminding him that there was "a child with no candy" somewhere.

laboratory＝研究室　apparent＝明らか

pp.24-25 / テレビの中で

① ...As you can see, a small miracle has happened here on the deserted northwest side of Everville. People are returning to this once well-known shopping district. A twenty-nine-year-old man, Ed Wishbone, has started a small pie shop in the ruins of an old trailer. This is his kitchen. He says that all of his utensils are fully sanitized and everything is safe and clean. Let's ask Mr. Wishbone himself about his pies.

Do you really make these pies in that backyard? They're really good. Sweet... but not too sweet.

Uh... thank you.

Are you thinking of entering the state pie festival this weekend?

Pie festival?

The Annual State Pie Festival is held this year at the Everville Mall. You should consider entering. The prize this year is twenty thousand dollars!

I... I don't know. I really...

YEAH!!

② I think your customers know.

③ So now you've seen it, one man's journey to save the old streets of Everville. And from the way people are gathering, who knows? He just might succeed. This is Glen Hamperton reporting from Ever...

　ニュースの英語というのは実に独特です。基本的に書き言葉の英語に近いのですが、ひとつの文章に入っている情報量があまりに多いため、最初は戸惑うかもしれません。これは主役や脇役にまるまる一文、長い説明的な化粧文がついていることがよくあるからです。数行の間に状況をすべて説明しないといけないニュースでは、チャンスがあれ

ZOMBIE PIES
ADULTS HATE US!
BUT THEIR KIDS SURE LOVE US!
GLASSVIEW/STANDPOINT/EVERVILLE/BARDEL
WORLD'S ONE AND ONLY THEME PIE SHOP!

ば、文中のどこにでも情報を入れてきます。本文中ではエドが「29歳の男性」であることを、**Ed Wishbone** という名前の化粧品として無理やり「**twenty-nine-year-old man**」とくっつけて説明しています（①）。でも、こういう情報の部分を切り離すと、ニュースの文というのは意外なほど平易で、難しそうに見えても、実はとても単純です。レポーターの最初のセリフも、詰め込まれた情報の部分を削除してみると、これだけになってしまいます。

　A miracle has happened in Everville. People are coming back to Ghost Avenue. Ed Wishbone has started a pie shop here. This is his kitchen. He says all his utensils are clean. Let's ask Mr. Wishbone.

　この内容にできる限り具体的な情報を化粧品や付録の形でつけて、ドラマチックに仕立て上げると（「**this once well-known**／かつて有名だった」をつけるなど）、左のようなセリフになるというわけです。

　最後の③は、ニュースの現場から中継をスタジオに戻す時の決まり文句のオンパレードで、**CNN**（Cable News Network）などを見ていれば、年中耳に入ってきます。最後に軽いオチをつけて、レポーターが名前を言いながらしめくくるのがアメリカのニュースの伝統的な形式ですが、この時よく使われる決まり文句に **who knows?** というのがあります。分かりにくければ、まるごと消してしまっても文章の意味は通じます。「誰が（可能性がないと）言えよう？」と視聴者に問いかけることで、「あるいは可能性があるかも」とほのめかす言い方です。似たようなもので「**God only knows.**（神のみぞ知る）」というもう少しポピュラーな言い方もありますが、こちらは「可能性はあるが、かなり絶望的」というニュアンスを持っています。

　ちなみに、途中レポーターがもらす「**I think your customers know.**」（②）はごくふつうの文であることから、レポーターとしてではなく、一人の人間としての感情的なコメントだと分かります。

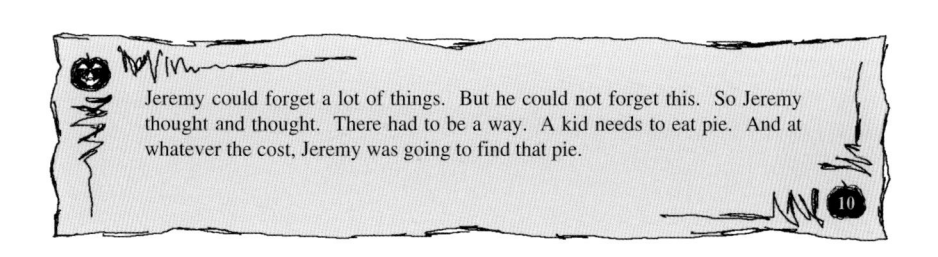

Jeremy could forget a lot of things. But he could not forget this. So Jeremy thought and thought. There had to be a way. A kid needs to eat pie. And at whatever the cost, Jeremy was going to find that pie.

pp.26-27 / ジェレミー親子の事情　その2

① This is bad. We can't afford having this man become any more popular than he is now.

Yes sir.

② As for this pie festival... You might as well have that chance of yours. Stop this man from winning the contest and perhaps I will reconsider the termination of your enterprise.

Will... will you really...

③ Do you, or do you not, want a chance?

④ Yes, sir. I'll try my best.

Your best is far from enough. Try harder.

Billy Bob, come here.

It's okay. I'm used to it. Nothing new.

　冒頭のジェレミーの父親のセリフ（①）で、少し変わった矢印が登場します。この「afford」は本来「○○を買うことができる」という意味でよく使われる言葉です。具体的な例をあげれば、何か高価なものを買おうという時に、店頭で迷った結果、夫が妻に

Early the next morning, a child named Archie Donnaheim awoke in bed, still holding the pamphlet his mother had brought him. He cried to sleep last night looking at the pamphlet. He knew that he would never go to Zombie Pies. He woke up from bed and looked out of his third-floor window.

「買ってもだいじょうぶだろうか？」と聞くと、妻がそれに答えて **"We can afford it."** というように使います。これは直訳すると「私たちはそれを買うことができる」という意味ですが、「それを買うだけの代償（ここでは「お金」）を払ってもだいじょうぶです」というのが本当の意味合いです。このセリフでは「**afford** できない」と否定の形になっているので、「エドが有名になる」ということがジェレミーの父親にとっては「払うことのできない代償」なのだと分かります。

　You might as well（②）という言い回しも一種の決まり文句ですが、分かりにくいようなら単純に **You can** か **You may** に置き換えてみてください。意味は同じですが、この回りくどい言い方はかなりえらそうな響きがあると同時に、「**well**」という部分に、「妥協の末、仕方なく」というニュアンスが含まれています。日本語にも似たようなものがあって、それは「いいだろう」という言葉です。これは確かに了承の言葉にはちがいないのですが、どこか「やむを得ないので仕方なく」という意味が含まれているのと同時に、上の者が下の者に言っている印象があります。

　中盤にもうひとつ難しい言い回しが出てきます（③）。「**Do you, or do you not, want a chance?**」は本来「**Do you want a chance, or do you not want a chance?**」ですが、切れのいいセリフにするため、ジェレミーの父親があえて最小限まで省略しています。イライラしているのがよく分かるセリフです。

　シーンの最後にはちょっと面白い言葉遊びが出てきます（④）。「**I'll try my best.**」というのは、謙虚にやる気を表明する時の決まり文句なのですが、ここではジェレミーの父親がそれに対して「おまえのベストじゃ足りない」と皮肉で返しています。

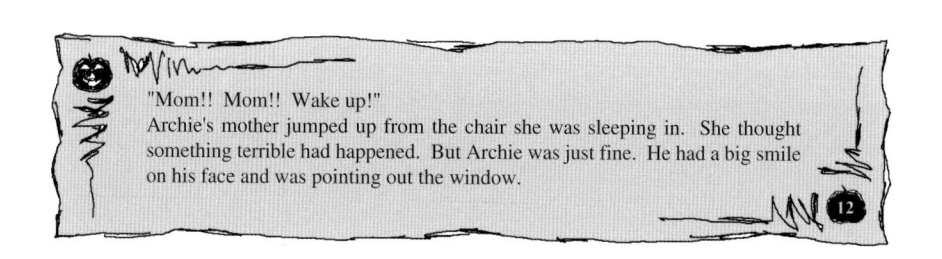

"Mom!! Mom!! Wake up!"
Archie's mother jumped up from the chair she was sleeping in. She thought something terrible had happened. But Archie was just fine. He had a big smile on his face and was pointing out the window.

pp.28-29 / エドとジョージの日常

> Now, *that* is something you don't see everyday.

① Damned if I'm seeing that.

Frank's good with animals, that's for sure.

② That's not an animal. That's a beast.

③ Yo, Ed. Apples done, man. What next?

Wow. You're getting faster everyday. Well... maybe you can help Willy and Pad clean the ovens.

④ Sure thing.

ジョージの最初のセリフに出てくる Damned（①）は『ビッグ・ファット・キャットとゴースト・アベニュー』にも登場した強調の言葉ですが、「このすごい光景が現実に見える」というジョージの強いおどろきを表現しています。分かりにくいのは、これも決まり文句だからです。

このページでも「単語のアップグレード」を使って、エドが皮肉を言っています（②）。animal → beast のアップグレードは日本語に直しても通じます。確かにエドの猫は「動物」というよりは「獣」に近いかもしれません。

ジョージは時々文末に man をつけて話していますが（③）、この man 自体にはほとんど意味がありません。日本語の「ったく」などと同じで、大変ポピュラーな英語の口癖です。あえて言うならリズムをとるために入っているような言葉です。

Sure thing.（④）は Sure. と意味はほとんど同じなのですが、Gotcha. と同様に、「任せとけ」という感じのある言葉です。

Archie's mother couldn't believe her eyes. Outside the window, there was a set just like the inside of Zombie Pies floating in the air. Someone had used a crane to build a giant landscape outside the window. And before she could say anything, the door opened and Zombie Pies music poured in.

13

crane＝クレーン車　landscape＝地形

Big Fat Cat and the Magic Pie Shop

pp.30-33 / ケンカとスラング

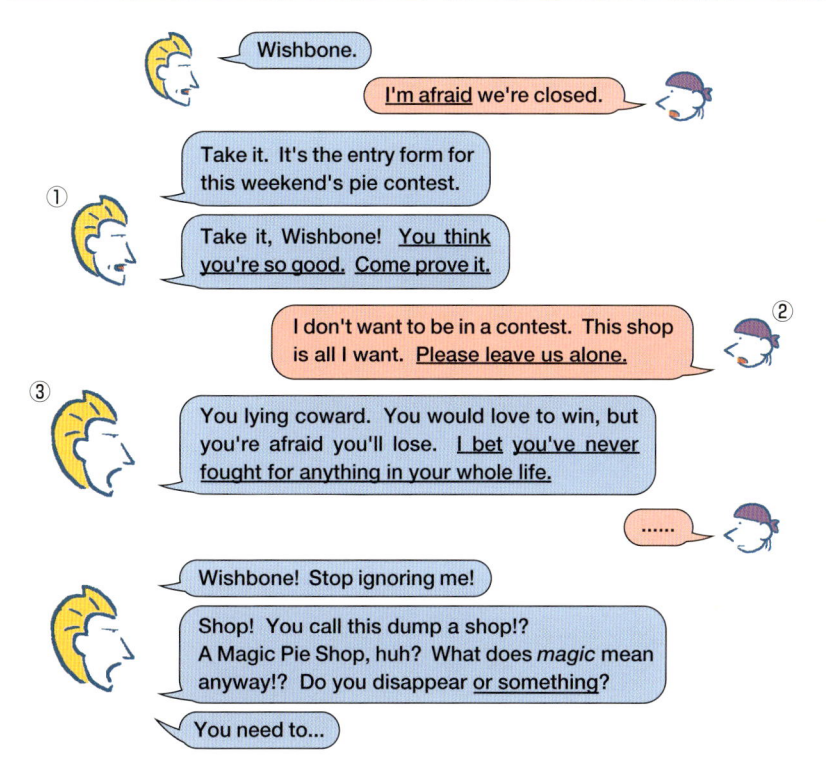

Wishbone.

I'm afraid we're closed.

Take it. It's the entry form for this weekend's pie contest.

① Take it, Wishbone! You think you're so good. Come prove it.

② I don't want to be in a contest. This shop is all I want. Please leave us alone.

③ You lying coward. You would love to win, but you're afraid you'll lose. I bet you've never fought for anything in your whole life.

……

Wishbone! Stop ignoring me!

Shop! You call this dump a shop!? A Magic Pie Shop, huh? What does *magic* mean anyway!? Do you disappear or something?

You need to...

　ここはケンカのシーンです。日本語でもそうですが、英語のケンカにも決まり文句がたくさんあります。頭に血が上っている時には冷静に考えられないので、浮かんだ決まり文句を連発しがちです。このシーンのジェレミーなどは正にそうです。

　英語のケンカで相手を挑発する時に、よく出てくるのが **prove** という矢印です（①）。

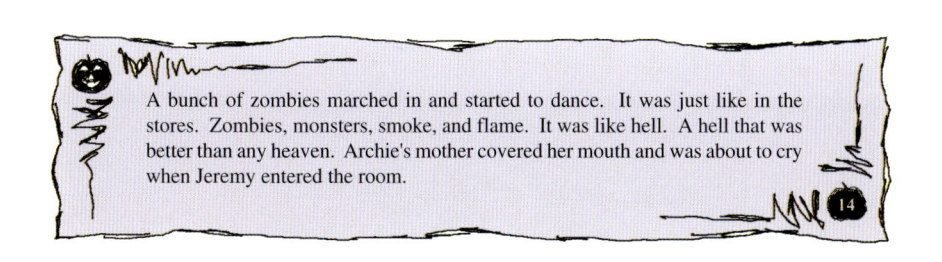

A bunch of zombies marched in and started to dance. It was just like in the stores. Zombies, monsters, smoke, and flame. It was like hell. A hell that was better than any heaven. Archie's mother covered her mouth and was about to cry when Jeremy entered the room.

14

合理主義のアメリカらしい考え方ですが、とにかく「証拠を見せろ」と迫るわけです。

　bet は **prove** と並ぶケンカ用の矢印です（③）。「I bet」というのは皮肉で、「賭けてもいいが、そうだろ」と相手を挑発しています。

　それに対して、エドの **leave us (me) alone**（②）はいじめられる側の決まり文句です。もちろん本当に一人になりたいわけではなく、「ほっといて」という意味です。これらはどれも小学校の運動場で実によく聞く言い回しです。

What are you...

Take your foot off my shop!

It's just a sign...

I said, take it off! ④

Hey... you don't need to...

You're just like me.

⑤ What?

Are you <u>out of your mind</u>!? I'm exactly not like you! I'm rich, I'm smart, I'm... rich, I'm...

You don't know what a pie is made of.

This man is <u>out of his mind</u>. You kicked him too much!

⑥ <u>What do you know!?</u>
<u>What the fuck do you know!?</u>

What...

"Zombie Pies at you service, ma'am. Our motto is one pie to one child. So if you can't come to us, we'll come to you! And Archie, here's your special pie!" Jeremy said and gave Archie a pie box. Archie's mother stepped forward in alarm, but Jeremy smiled at her.
"You have nothing to worry." ⑮

motto ＝モットー

そして、ケンカの時の決まり文句と言えば、なんといってもスラングです。このスラングと呼ばれる一連の（たいてい下品な）俗語は、なかなか参考書で紹介されることはありません。それはほとんどのスラングの元の意味が卑猥なものか、暴力的なものか、人種差別的なものだからだということもありますが、それ以上に、日本語にはスラングに相当する言葉がないので、説明が極めてしにくいということもあります。

　アメリカに行ってみればすぐに気がつくことですが、スラングはとても日常的に使われています。にも関わらず、アメリカ国内でも、学校でスラングを教えたりすることはなく（むしろ、全面的に禁止しているのがふつうです）、辞書にもほとんど掲載されていません。

　ジェレミーがとっさに使ってしまった **fuck**（⑥）という単語が、スラングのもっとも代表的なもののひとつで（すでにおなじみの **damn** もそうです）、ハリウッドのアクション映画を見ていれば、何度も聞くことができる単語です。

　この **fuck** という言葉はスラングとして使われる時にはほとんど意味はなく、どこにどう使っても極めて強い強調になります。日本語に訳される時には対応する言葉がないため、仕方なく「くそ」とか「畜生」になっていますが、それではこの単語のインパクトは表現できません。

　fuck という単語のもたらすインパクトは、日本語では説明が不可能です。どうしても想像したい方は、自分が知っているもっとも口に出せない単語を想像してみてください。それをふつうの会話の中で、化粧品として使うような感じだと言えば、少しは伝わるでしょうか。

　とにかく、常識のある一般人がこの単語を発してしまう時は、もはや後先が考えられないほど頭に血が上っている時だということだけは覚えておいてください。しょっちゅう耳にするにも関わらず、これは本当に一種の「禁句」なのです。

　ジェレミーの父親が使っていた「**I said**」で繰り返す形を、ここではエドが使っていま

"But..."
Archie opened the box with eyes twinkling with joy. Inside was a carefully shaped mold of jellos tangled together with red and yellow sugar on top.
"Behold, the Bloody Slimeyard!! And don't worry. There's nothing in there that's bad. I checked with the doctor," Jeremy said.

twinkling ＝輝く　mold ＝固まり　jellos ＝ゼリー

す（④）。大事な看板を壊されて、エドもよほど怒っているのが分かります。

　I'm exactly not like you.（⑤）はちょっと面白い文です。ふつうは **exactly** はつきません。日本語でも「ぴったりちがう」というのがないのと同じです。でも、ここではジェレミーはエドに言われたことがよほど気に障ったのか、わざわざ **exactly** を使って、無理やり否定しています（日本語だと「これ以上ないくらいにちがう」などになるでしょうか）。なんでも **not** をつければ否定になってしまう英語の手軽さを使ったセリフです。ジェレミーもエドの鋭い言葉に内心ドキッとしたのかもしれません。

pp.35-36 / ケンカのてんまつ

① That's enough.
② See you at the contest.
③ Ed! Man! You all right?
George... I'm sorry.
Hey man, it's just a sign. I'll paint you another one tomorrow.
Magic ain't in the sign, man. Cheer up! We won!
YEAH!!

Archie could not wait and was already holding a spoon.
"Mom. Mom, may I...!?"
Archie's mother could not stop crying. She thought she would never be able to say this answer.
"Yes. Yes, Archie. You may."

17

That's enough. (①) の That は何なのかと考えると、かえって難しくなります。厳密に言えば、That は「BB がしていたこと（エドに暴力をふるう）」を「enough（十分）」だと言って止めているのですが、実際にはこの That's はあってもなくてもかまいません。"Enough!" という言葉が単独で「決まり文句」になっているからです。ケンカなどを止めたり、やりすぎている誰かを制したりする時に、叫ぶような形で使うことが多いのですが、ここではより強調するために、ちゃんとした文にしています。この時、一番簡単に主役に当てはめられるのが何の代役にでもなる that だったというだけです。

　本編ではジェレミーは二番目のセリフ（②）を言った直後に去っていきます。これは俗に言う「捨てゼリフ」です。こういったセリフは短い方がかっこいいという理由と、弱い命令口調にする意味を込めて、主役の I'll が文から抜け落ちています。

　ここでのジョージのセリフは彼らしくアレンジされています。最初のセリフの You all right?（③）は本来 Are you all right? です。最後の文の ain't は本当なら isn't ですが、地方などでは時々このように変形して使われていることがあります。ジョージは小さなことは気にしません。ちょっとくらいの間違いは誰でもしてしまうもの——ジョージにとっては、言い間違いも十分個性です。

　それよりもエドがはじめて相手に立ち向かったのですから、ジョージが言っている通り、Cheer up! するべきでしょう！　ここで使われている矢印の cheer は歓喜の声をあげたり、応援したりすることを指していますが、その声を up —— 高らかにせよと言っているのですから、転じて「元気を出せ！」という意味の決まり文句です。Yeah!

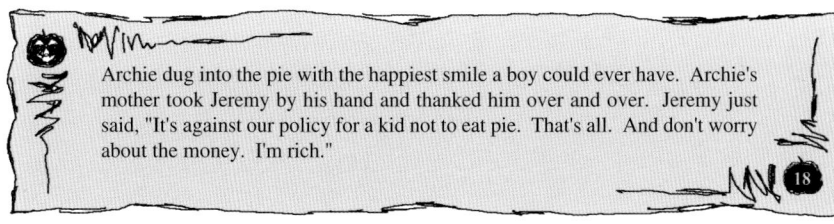

Archie dug into the pie with the happiest smile a boy could ever have. Archie's mother took Jeremy by his hand and thanked him over and over. Jeremy just said, "It's against our policy for a kid not to eat pie. That's all. And don't worry about the money. I'm rich."

policy＝ポリシー

pp.37-39 / 単語のアップグレード　その2

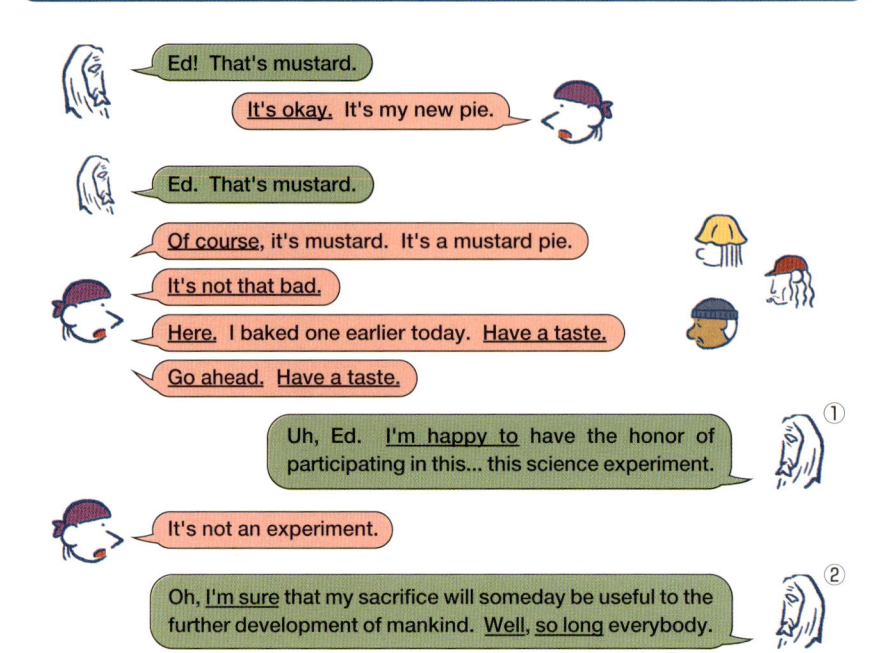

- Ed! That's mustard.
- It's okay. It's my new pie.

- Ed. That's mustard.
- Of course, it's mustard. It's a mustard pie.
- It's not that bad.
- Here. I baked one earlier today. Have a taste.
- Go ahead. Have a taste.

① Uh, Ed. I'm happy to have the honor of participating in this... this science experiment.

- It's not an experiment.

② Oh, I'm sure that my sacrifice will someday be useful to the further development of mankind. Well, so long everybody.

　このシーンでは Willy が「単語のアップグレード」を行って、みんなの笑いを取っています。ふつうなら I'll try the pie. と言うところを honor、participating、science experiment など、受賞スピーチにでも出てきそうな単語を織り交ぜることで、思いきり大げさな言い方に仕立て上げています（①）。

　「単語のアップグレード」はここまでにも数回登場していますが、面白い会話には不可欠な要素です。英語は日本語のようにしゃべり方に種類がありません。「男性のしゃべり

Archie smiled to his mother with a big spoonful of purple and pink slime dripping off his mouth. Zombie Pies music was loud in the room.
Archie's mother thought that "The Bloody Slimeyard Pie" was the most horrible, disgusting and most wonderful pie she ever saw in her life.
END ⑲

disgusting ＝吐き気のする

方(「こんなしゃべり方か？」)」「女性のしゃべり方(こういうしゃべり方かしら？)」「おじいさん、おばあさんのしゃべり方(こんなしゃべり方のことかのう？)」など、日本語のしゃべり方は年齢、性別、社会的背景などによってかなり特色がある上、「敬語」というシステムもあり、セリフに感情を反映しやすくなっています。

ところが英語はどんな年齢や性別の人でも、セリフ自体にはそこまで大きな差が出てきません。そこで、個性を出すために「言葉選び」が重要になってきます。今まで紹介してきた「決まり文句」のうち、どれを自分のものとして採用するかというのも「言葉選び」のひとつですが、単語レベルでも、「この単語の持っているイメージは自分に合っているかどうか」と考えながら選んでいくと、しゃべり方にも個性が出ます。特に役者や矢印などは、同じ意味を持つ単語が複数用意されていることがよくあるので、そのどれを選んで日常的に使うかで、かなりその人のイメージが決まります。たとえば「言う」を意味する矢印の種類を考えてみましょう。

say / speak / tell / state / suggest / mention / remark / pronounce

はっきりした順番はありませんが、一般的に単語が長く複雑になっていくほど、「頭がいい」「大げさ」「強調」「権威」などのイメージを伴います。これは、そういった単語があまり日常的に使われないものだからです。本編の冒頭でもエドたちが何度か、**attack**、**kill**などの日常あまり耳にしない単語を持ち出して、大げさなことを言っているシーンがありました。物語中盤ではジェレミーの父親がわざと難しい単語を並べ立てて相手を威圧したしゃべり方をしています。このページでもウィリーが本来なら **I'll try the pie.** というだけのことを、**Uh, Ed.** で始まる大げさなセリフに拡大して(①、②)、みんなを笑わせています。

このように「言葉選び」は英語に欠かせない重要な要素です。ただ、どの単語にどういうイメージがあるかは辞書には載っていません。物語の中で出てくるのを待って、無意識に自分の中でイメージを作っていくしかありません。でも、それが楽しいのです！

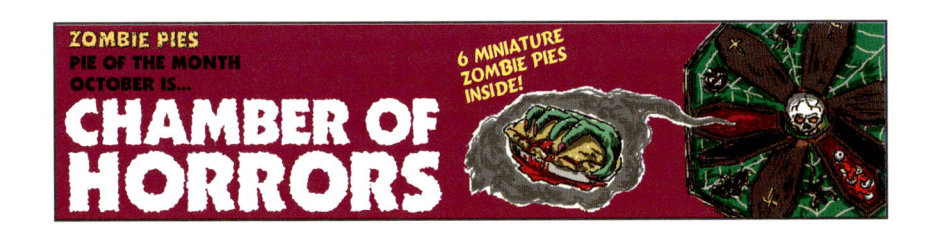

pp.39-41 / 緊迫したシーンでの決まり文句

① The smell!? Just with the smell!? No way!!

I'm telling you! It's not that bad!

Hey, Willy. You can get up now. We got your point. Willy?

No! It's not the pie! It's his heart! It's doing it again!

What?

② Prof! C'mon! Prof!

③ BeeJees! What the hell is going on!?

Don't worry. It's not your pie. Willy's heart is in a real bad condition.

Why isn't he in a hospital?

Because hospitals cost money.

Use mine.

Hospital costs lots of money. At least two grand a week. And that's without any treatment.

He's not responding!

Oh no... This is bad, man. This is really bad.

Burbert, do you think there really are UFOs?

I doubt it, sir.

But maybe! Just maybe! I have this feeling.

I don't know why, but I just believe in UFOs.

No way（①）もポピュラーな決まり文句です。**no** というのは、かなり強い言い方です。ホラー映画などで化け物に追いつめられたキャラクターが殺される直前に叫ぶのがたいてい **NOOO!** であるように、信じられないほど恐ろしい光景を目撃してしまった時に、口から自然に出る言葉です。だから、友達間などで何かを断る場合に **no** を使うと、少しきつい感じを相手に与えてしまいます。それを和らげるために使われる言い方のひとつがこの **no way** です。日本語に直すなら、一番近いニュアンスの言い方は「無理だよー」と照れながら、少し強く否定する感じでしょうか。

　逆にセリフに **no** が単独で出てきた時は、かなり強い否定と考えるべきです。今回も何度か出てきていますので、探し出して、どんな時に使われているか確認してみてください。

　I'm telling you（①）も決まり文句です。「言ってるだろ！」と、なかなか分かってくれない人に強く確認する時によく使われます。「**I said**」で自分が言ったことを繰り返すのにも似ていますが、そちらが命令的なのに対して、こちらは説得している感じです。この場面でエドがこちらを選んだのは、相手が仲間だったからでしょう。

　そして、再び **C'mon** の登場です（②）。ここではビージーズが意識を失ったウィリーに呼びかけるために使っています。「こっちの世界に戻ってこい」という意味の **C'mon** です。このあとも **C'mon** は何度か登場します。近くにいる人に呼びかけるだけでなく、意見のちがう人、ちがう世界に行ってしまった人など、あらゆる意味で自分から「離れている」人に呼びかける時に使える、実に便利な決まり文句がこの **C'mon** です。

　hell（③）は **fuck** ほどではないのですが、かなり強い強調のスラングです。キリスト教の国では「地獄」という意味の言葉は、日本人が考えているよりはるかにインパクトがあります。ただ、**fuck** とちがって、**hell** 自体は禁止用語ではありません。気軽に使ってはいけない言葉だというだけです。

pp.41-43 / 言っていい人、悪い人

- Isn't there a phone somewhere? We need an ambulance.
- You know there isn't a single working phone on this street. <u>Besides</u>..., no ambulance would come here <u>at this time of night.</u>
- Then <u>what are we supposed to do</u>? <u>He's dying, isn't he?</u>
- Pray.
- We have to get him to a hospital.
- Don't!
- ① Why not!? <u>For heaven's sake!</u>
- He wanted to die, Wishbone. If he's going to die, let him die here.
- <u>That's insane!</u>
- ② Wishbone. You're just making this harder. <u>Let him go.</u>
- <u>C'mon</u> and help me. We have to get him to a hospital.
- <u>I'm telling you</u>, Wishbone. You're just increasing everyone's pain. ③
- I know I'm naive. I just don't want to give up. I've given up too many things already.
- <u>Damn it</u>, Wishbone. Why can't you understand? <u>It's too late.</u> We're all too late. ④

Ed's easy to learn Cooking Kitchen

TODAY'S RECIPE
Grasshopper Pie
A cold chocolate mint pie!

Big Fat Cat and the Magic Pie Shop

　ウィリーが倒れてしまい、緊迫した雰囲気の中、エドとビージーズの意見が激しくぶつかるシーンです。エドもビージーズもウィリーのためを思って言っているのですが、それぞれの育ちと経験のちがいから、どうしても異なる結論に達してしまいます。

　日本で「救急車が来ない」というのはまず考えられないことですが、アメリカでは治安の悪い地区は危険すぎて、救急隊員も命がけなので、十分にあり得る話です。

　ここで「決まり文句」の **For heaven's sake**（①）が登場します。基本的にはその直前の **Why not!?** という疑問に対する強調です。とにかく最大級にその思いを強調したい時、キリスト教の国では天国や地獄を持ち出してくると強い印象を与えます。「神の国の威信に賭けて、いったいなぜだー！？」と叫びたくなるほど、エドは「病院に連れて行くな」というビージーズの言葉に耳を疑ったにちがいありません。

　物語もここへ来て、今までに出てきた「決まり文句」がいくつか再登場しています。**C'mon**（②）、**Damn it.**（④）などは本当に良く登場する言葉です。注目したいのは以前エドが使っていた **I'm telling you.**（③）という「決まり文句」をビージーズが使っていることです。エドとビージーズは二人ともそれほどケンカを好む性格ではないため、こういう緊迫した場面で選べる言葉は自然と限られてきます。この **I'm telling you.** は「言っているだろう」という、どこか優等生的な脅し文句なので、**BFC** シリーズのキャラクターの中でも、使う人と使わない人がはっきり分かれます。

使いそうな人	微妙な人	使いそうもない人

　この図からも分かるように、「決まり文句」というのは本当にそれぞれはっきりしたイメージを持っています。むしろその意味よりも、イメージの方が大事だと言っても過言ではないかもしれません。

Ingredients
(for the crust)
1 3/4 cup chocolate cookies
1/3 cup melted butter or margarine
(for the filling)
1/2 cup milk

32 large marshmallows
1 tablespoon cacao liqueur
1 3/4 cup whipped cream
few drops mint essence
a sprinkle of green food color
chocolate spray

pp.45-47 / yes と no の距離感

① <u>No way</u> we can repair this.

<u>I guess</u> we'll have to carry the cart.

Maybe I can carry Willy on my back.

② <u>It... might not be a good idea</u> to rock him too much. <u>Besides</u> we still have a mile to go. Can you take the front end? I'll get the back.

③ <u>No problem.</u>

最初は **No way**（①）の再登場です。しかし、この場合は本当に「修理する方法（way）がない」と言っているので、ふつうの文に近い形になっています。

Willy?

He's... singing.

④ Singing? <u>Oh, yeah.</u> I hear it too.

It might not be a good idea（②）というのは、やはり no という言い方を和らげた言い回しのひとつです。ジョージの提案をやんわりと否定しています。

ジョージのセリフ「**No problem.**」（③）も、英語の決まり文句の中でもっともよく登場するもののひとつで、**Gotcha.** や **Sure thing.** などと並んで、より強い yes の形です。

最後の **Oh, yeah.**（④）はかなり乱暴な返事です。ジョージはふだんは **No problem.** のような、もっとやわらかい言い方を使うのですが、ここでは疲れきっているために、気を使えなかったのでしょう。

yes と **no** 自体は、そのままの形では意外なほど使われていません。このページから、それがよく分かると思います。

---

1. Heat oven to 180℃. Crush the chocolate cookies into crumbs. Mix crumbs and melted butter. Press mixture firmly against bottom and side of pie plate. Bake about 10 minutes, then cool.

p.49 / What a Wonderful World

I see trees of green, red roses too
I watch them bloom for me and you
And I think to myself
What a wonderful world

I see skies of blue, clouds of white
The bright blessed day and the dark sacred night
And I think to myself
What a wonderful world

I hear babies cry, I watch them grow
They'll learn much more than I'll ever know
And I think to myself
What a wonderful world
Yes I think to myself
What a wonderful world

　もうろうとする意識の中、見上げた夜空がよほど美しかったのか、ウィリーは無意識に名曲、**What a Wonderful World**（作詞・作曲／**George David Weiss & Bob Thiele**）を口ずさみ始めます。これを歌った **Louis Armstrong** は「サッチモ」の愛称で世界中に親しまれた偉大なジャズミュージシャンです。彼の晩年の代表作となったこの曲は、世界の根源的な美しさを歌った **1967** 年の作品で、日本でもテレビのコマーシャルなどでたびたび流れています。タイトルに心当たりがなくても、メロディーを聴けば、「ああ、あの曲か」と思う方も多いはずです。機会があれば、ぜひ聴いてみてください。

2. Heat milk and marshmallows in saucepan over low heat, stirring constantly, until marshmallows are melted. Refrigerate about 20 minutes, stirring occasionally. Gradually stir in cacao liqueur and mint essence.

pp.50-53 / 「上の階」に任せるということ

> Someone! Someone, help us! We need help!

> Ma'am, we need help.

> Please. We need a doctor. If it's money, I have some. And I promise I'll get more in a few days.

> No! Please! We really need help! Here! This is all the money I have now, but...!!

> Please... we...

> At least we tried, man.

> I bet the Prof's happy too. Yo, man. Maybe it's time to give up. Leave things to good old Jesus upstairs. ①

> Yo, c'mon Ed.

> Yo. Let's go home. I think Willy's just sleeping. He'll be fine until tomorrow morning.

　現実の冷たさを思い知らされたエドは、病院の扉の前で力なく崩れ落ちます。ビージーズもかつて同じ経験があったので、エドたちを止めたのかもしれません。エドもジョージもふらふらなためか、セリフは「決まり文句」だらけです。もはや考える力がなくて、頭に浮かんだことを次々に言っているだけなので、これは当然のことです。

---

3. Beat whipping cream in chilled bowl until stiff. Mix marshmallow mixture into whipped cream. Add food color. Spread in crust. Sprinkle with chocolate. Refrigerate about 4 hours.

ここで印象的なセリフはなんといっても、ジョージの二つ目のセリフ（①）です。「ギブアップしよう」と絶望的な提案をしながらも、その言葉にはどこか明るさがあります。「upstairs（上の階）」にいる「Jesus（イエス＝キリスト）」にあとは任せるということも、アメリカでは選択肢のひとつに入ります。ジョージやエドは決して敬虔なキリスト教徒ではありません。子供の時からキリスト教に深く根ざした教育を受け、キリスト教がとけ込んだ社会で生きているので、やはり追いつめられるとこういう言葉が当たり前に出てくるのでしょう。

　ちゃんとした家なら日曜日は教会に行くのが当たり前とされる国——それがアメリカです。アメリカの小説を読む時には、その要素を無視して通ることはできません。しかし、アメリカでのキリスト教というのは日本の宗教のイメージとはだいぶちがっていて、社会道徳の一部ともいえる、一般的な思想です。アメリカに旅行に行く機会があったら、日曜日に教会に行ってみると、アメリカ人のことがもっとよく分かるようになります。

　これまでいろんな「決まり文句」を見てきましたが、やはり「決まり文句」の中にはキリスト教と切っても切れない関係のものが数多く含まれています。キリスト教の基本的な事柄だけでも学んでおくと、いろいろな本や映画に隠された謎を解くヒントになることもありますよ！

「英語をしゃべる」ということの正体

　こういう時にはこう言う —— 日常の会話の中には、「決まり文句」というものが無意識に使われています。解説の最初でも書きましたが、これらは呪文のようなものです。その呪文を唱えると、どんな効果が現れるかが、ある程度決められた言葉たちです。
　「Pardon me?」と唱えれば、相手は今言ったことを繰り返してくれますし、「Sure thing.」と唱えれば、いい返事をもらえたのだと安心してくれます。
　呪文というのは分かれば便利なものですが、知らないで聞くと、ひどく意味の分からないものに聞こえてしまうこともあります。それもそのはずで、何度も繰り返し使っているうちに、意味が激しく変わってしまったものなどもあるからです（「**For heaven's sake!**」「**God bless you.**」など）。

　でも、頭の中で文を作りながら同時にしゃべるというのは母国語でも大変なことです。よく使うセリフは覚えてしまえば、会話の中で楽に使うことができます。また、まちがったイメージを相手に与える危険性を少なくすることにもなります。だから自分らしい「決まり文句」をたくさん持っていると、会話をするのが怖くなくなります。
　では、どうやってその「決まり文句」をためていくのかというと、見つけた「決まり文句」を全部リストにして、上から順に覚えていっても、あまり意味はありません。あふれるまで文や言い回しをためると、その中からよく使うものが少しずつ自分の決まり文

句に変化していきます。それがその人の「決まり文句」のリストに登録され、いつしか「その人らしい」言葉として周りに認知されていきます。この本の中では当たり前のように「決まり文句」に線を引いていますが、本当ははじめから決められた「決まり文句」なんてありません。「決める」のは、いつも自分なのですから。

自分だけの言葉

　エドにしても、ジェレミーにしても、みんな自分だけの決まり文句のリストを持っています。そして、そのリストはひとつとして同じものがありません。たとえば、誰かをほめるにしても、『ビッグ・ファット・キャットとマジック・パイ・ショップ』の登場人物たちはそれぞれにちがうほめ方をするはずです。

- Great!
- Good job!
- Way to go!
- Nice.
- Not bad.
- Well done. / Sufficient.
- ……

　英語にはいろんな種類の決まり文句があります。でも、くどいようですが、全部を覚える必要はありません。なぜなら、ほとんどの決まり文句は意味を考えなくても、前後の状況とその人の性格を考えると、何を言っているのか見当がつくようになっているか

らです。だからこそ「決まり文句」とも言えるのです。

　そして、どの決まり文句がどういうイメージを持っているかというのを、理屈で覚えるのは不可能に近いことです。たとえば「**Gotcha!**」は「兄貴肌で思い込みの強い、でも、楽天的で物事を深く考えないタイプの人が使う了承の言葉」と覚えようとしても、覚えられるはずがありません。**Gotcha!** をほかで見つけたら、「そういえばジョージが使っていたな」と考える方がずっと楽で、ずっと簡単なはずです。物語で英語を覚えていく強みはなんといってもここにあります。

　これからはセリフの中で分からないものが出てきたら、「どうせ決まり文句だろう」と心を楽にして、場面の雰囲気から何を言っているのか想像してみたり、単語の字面から推測してみたり、それでもだめだったらとばしてみたりするのも手です。

　相手も同じ人間です。ある場面である状況に遭遇した時、そんなにちがうことを感じたり考えたり、ましてや言ったりはしません。おそらくその決まり文句は、あなたが同じ立場になった時に言ってしまう言葉と、似たような意味のものになるはずです。ただ、人それぞれぴったりくる言い方がちがうだけです。セリフは難しそうに見えても、落ち着いてよく考えれば、なんとなく意味が見えてきます。

　難しい英語のセリフに遭遇した時は、頭ではなく、心で考えること ―― それこそが英会話の唯一にして最大のコツなのかもしれません。

BFC EXTRA SPECIAL

ZOMBIE PIES

REGULAR MENU

ZOMBIE
ADULTS HATE US!

THE PIE FROM HELL
This classic evil blood-red cherry pie will grab your heart out!

$22.95 — THE ORIGINAL!

"EYE SEE YOU"
Is that eyeball looking at you? Don't be so sure. Eat them all! The greatest cream puffs!

$22.95 — COMES WITH "EYE'S CREAM"

MELTING ICEMAN
Light those candles and watch berry-flavored iceman melt over your ice cream pie!

$22.95 — GREAT FOR PARTIES!

WITCH'S BREW
This black cheese filled pie is haunted by Wocka the Witch and her cat!

$24.95 — WOCKA FLIES!!

GHOST IN THE BOX
Open the 9 doors to random selected flavor pies of the month! But beware, one contains the Red Hot Zombie Blood!

$26.95 — ALL NEW PIE!

PIES
BUT THEIR KIDS SURE LOVE US!

ALIEN EGG
Inside the purple alien egg, four different fillings await you!

$29.95

CRACK IT AND SEE!

GREEN SLIME BUCKET
Scoop a big dip of mint slime into your cup of crust!

$24.95

COMPLETE WITH DIPPER!

GRAVEYARD DIG
Dig into the graveyard with shovel spoons (included with pies)! Lucky kid finds the gold medal and gets a free slice of pie!

$24.95

#2 BESTSELLER!

『ビッグ・ファット・キャットとマジック・パイ・ショップ』の最後に

　『マジック・パイ・ショップ』へのご来店、ありがとうございました！　今回からリクエストにお応えして、三色辞典の「読むためのヒント集」も大幅に増やしてみました。ぜひそちらも合わせてご覧ください。

　解説の方は「決まり文句」にスポットをあててお送りしましたが、「決まり文句」だけでなく、単語にはそれぞれ、その単語の持つイメージがあります。

　たとえば cold の翻訳は「冷たい」ではありません。cold と聞いて、氷に触った時の指先の感覚が思い出せれば cold です。それを cold →「冷たい」→「あの感覚」という順番で訳していると、一拍入った日本語の感覚になってしまいます。フィルターを通しての cold になってしまいます。

　でも、最初はそれでいいんです。ほかに方法がありません。そのうちとても印象的な絵本で cold という単語が使われていて、そこに雪の日の絵が描いてあるのを目にすれば、cold から直接その絵が浮かぶようになってきます。そうしたら、やがてその絵のイメージがもっと抽象的な感覚として心の隅に残り、cold と聞いただけで体が寒くなります。

　「単語を覚える」というのはそういうことです。「cold ＝冷たい」を繰り返し記憶することではなく、cold という単語に思い出を作ってあげることです。「冷たい」という日本語に頼らなくてもいい思い出を。

　絵本が言語の勉強に適しているのは、単語に「思い出」を作りやすいメディアだからです。英語に詳しくなるというのは、すなわち英語の思い出がたくさんできることです。決して文法のルールをたくさん覚えることではありません。

　いい本をたくさん読んで、いい思い出をたくさん作ってください。

　それでは次回、パイ・フェスティバルの会場でお会いしましょう！

Good luck and happy reading!
向山貴彦

　当シリーズは英文法の教科書ではなく、あくまで「英語を読む」ことを最大の目的として作られています。そのため、従来の英文法とはいささか異なる解釈を用いている部分があります。これらの相違は英語に取り組み始めたばかりの方にも親しみやすくするため、あえて取り入れたものです。

STAFF

written and produced by Takahiko Mukoyama	企画・原作・文・解説 向山貴彦
illustrated by Tetsuo Takashima	絵・キャラクターデザイン たかしまてつを
rewritten by Tomoko Yoshimi	文章校正 吉見知子
art direction by Yoji Takemura	アートディレクター 竹村洋司
DTP by Aya Nakamura	DTP 中村文
technical advice by Takako Mukoyama	テクニカルアドバイザー 向山貴子
edited by Masayasu Ishihara Shoji Nagashima Atsushi Hino	編集 石原正康（幻冬舎） 永島賞二（幻冬舎） 日野淳（幻冬舎）
editorial assistance by Daisaku Takeda Kaori Miyayama	編集協力 武田大作 宮山香里
English-language editing by Michael Keezing	英文校正 マイクル・キージング（keezing.communications）
supportive design by Akira Hirakawa Miyuki Matsuda	デザイン協力 平川彰（幻冬舎デザイン室） 松田美由紀（幻冬舎デザイン室）
supervised by Atsuko Mukoyama Yoshihiko Mukoyama	監修 向山淳子（梅光学院大学） 向山義彦（梅光学院大学）
a studio ET CETERA production	製作 スタジオ・エトセトラ
published by GENTOSHA	発行 幻冬舎

special thanks to:
Mac & Jessie Gorham　マック＆ジェシー・ゴーハム
Baiko Gakuin University　梅光学院大学

series dedicated to "Fuwa-chan," our one and only special cat

BIG FAT CAT オフィシャルウェブサイト
http://www.studioetcetera.com/bigfatcat

幻冬舎ホームページ
http://www.gentosha.co.jp

WHAT A WONDERFUL WORLD
Word & Music by Bob Thiele, George David Weiss
©1967 by QUARTET MUSIC INC. / RANGE ROAD MUSIC INC. / ABILENE MUSIC INC.
All rights reserved. Used by permission.
Print rights for Japan jointly administered by YAMAHA MUSIC FOUNDATION &
FUJIPACIFIC MUSIC INC.
JASRAC　出 0312351-301

〈著者紹介〉
向山貴彦　1970年アメリカ・テキサス州生まれ。作家。製作集団スタジオ・エトセトラを創設。デビュー作『童話物語』(幻冬舎文庫)は、ハイ・ファンタジーの傑作として各紙誌から絶賛された。向山淳子氏、たかしまてつを氏との共著『ビッグ・ファット・キャットの世界一簡単な英語の本』は、英語修得のニュー・スタンダードとして注目を浴び、ミリオンセラーとなった。

たかしまてつを　1967年愛知県生まれ。フリーイラストレーターとして、雑誌等で活躍。1999年イタリアのボローニャ国際絵本原画展入選。著書に『ビッグ・ファット・キャットのグリーティング・カード』(幻冬舎文庫)。

ビッグ・ファット・キャットとマジック・パイ・ショップ
2003年10月25日　第1刷発行
2017年10月20日　第4刷発行

著　者　向山貴彦　たかしまてつを
発行者　見城　徹
発行所　株式会社 幻冬舎
　　　　〒151-0051 東京都渋谷区千駄ヶ谷4-9-7

電話:03(5411)6211(編集)
　　　03(5411)6222(営業)
振替:00120-8-767643
印刷・製本所:株式会社 光邦

検印廃止

万一、落丁乱丁のある場合は送料当社負担でお取替致します。小社宛にお送り下さい。本書の一部あるいは全部を無断で複写複製することは、法律で認められた場合を除き、著作権の侵害となります。定価はカバーに表示してあります。

©TAKAHIKO MUKOYAMA, TETSUO TAKASHIMA, GENTOSHA 2003
Printed in Japan
ISBN 4-344-00409-4 C0095
幻冬舎ホームページアドレス　http://www.gentosha.co.jp/

この本に関するご意見・ご感想をメールでお寄せいただく場合は、
comment@gentosha.co.jpまで。

BIG FAT CAT'S
3 COLOR
DICTIONARY

**BIG FAT CAT
and the
MAGIC PIE SHOP**

Big Fat Cat's 3 Color Dictionary

p.7 1. **You know this town**... A→B

1. 最初の四文の you はずばり読者のあなたです。エヴァーヴィルへおかえりなさい！

p.8 **You know this street**... A→B

p.10 And **you know this man**. A→B

p.11 But **some things have changed** since the last time you saw him. A↩

2. **It has been a long month** for Ed Wishbone. A=B

2. It はおなじみ「時間」の代役。物語冒頭の定番です。

p.12 3. "George! Cherry! We need more cherry!" **Ed shouted** as he **handed the last slice of cherry pie** to a customer.
A→B as A→B

3. ここでは cherry pies の pies を略しています。

4. **George was pulling a freshly baked banana chocolate pie out of the barrel oven.** A=B
He shouted to Ed. A↩
"Gotcha!" 不完全な文
George handed the pie over to Paddy and **started** running down the street to the old cinema. A→B and (A)→B

4. barrel oven がどんなものかは 14 ページの挿絵をごらんください。

5. **They kept several extra pies** there, just in case. A→B
6. "W-where do you want this?" **Paddy asked Ed**. A→B／B'

5. パイが足りなくなった case（場合）を想定して、extra pies を映画館に kept しています。just in case は「万が一」の意味の決まり文句です。

p.13 "Below the counter somewhere," **Ed told Paddy** hurriedly as **he turned** back to a waiting customer.
A→B／B' as A↩

6. this は「パディがジョージから受け取ったパイ」です。

7. "**I'm sorry**, ma'am. A=B
What **can I get** for you today?" A→B

7. ma'am は madam の略。女性に対するていねいな呼びかけ。男性の場合は sir。

8. "**I'll take a slice of that new lemon pie**... and of course, two slices of blueberry, as usual." A→B
"**That'll be 75 cents**." A=B
"**Are you sure**? A=B
I **feel** like I'm cheating you. A↩
Paying you only 75 cents for such a wonderful pie." 不完全な文
"**Thank you**. (A)→B
But **don't worry**. (A)↩
We're doing fine." A=B
"Well, God **bless** you. A→B

8. as usual は「時間」の付録。分かりにくければとばして読んでみてください。

9. **I hope** you can do something about this long waiting line though." A→B
"**I'm sorry**, ma'am. **I'll try**. A=B A↩
Have a nice day." (A)→B
"You too, now." 不完全な文

9. 長蛇の列に「do something」で「何か対処をする」。

10. Ed **ducked** down under the counter for a moment and **whispered** to Paddy. A↩ and (A)↩
    "I'm going to **check** the pies in the oven. A = B
    Watch the shop for me, okay, Pad?" (A) → B
    "Uh... I-I'm not **sure**, Ed." A = B
11. Paddy **looked** doubtful but Ed **was** already dashing out the side door. A = B but A = B
    Behind the trailer, there **was** a small outdoor kitchen. A = B
    Ed and George **had made** three ovens out of barrels, steel panels, and pieces of wire. A → B
    The smell of butter and sugar **was** everywhere. A = B
12. Willy and the cat **were** playing around while Frank watched nearby, sitting in an old toy wagon. A = B
    At least, Willy **was** playing. A = B
13. The cat's eyes **were** much more serious, focused on the pies in the oven. A = B

    Ed **spoke** to Willy as he **opened** the first oven and **peeked** inside. A↩ as A → B and (A) → B
14. "Will, please **keep** that cat out of the kitchen. A → B = B'
    It's not **clean**." A = B
15. "Oh, c'mon Ed. He deserves a piece, too," Willy **protested**. A → B
    "That cat already **ate** two whole pies this morning!" A → B
    Ed **pointed** his finger at the cat. A → B = B'
    The cat **paid** no attention. A → B
    BeeJees **grunted**. A↩
    He **was** sitting nearby on an old tractor tire. A = B
    "That cat **bit** me when I tried to pet him." A → B
    "Bit you?!" George **said**. A → B
16. He **had returned** from the theater with a cherry pie in his hands. A↩
17. He **was** still out of breath. A = B
18. He **showed** his free hand to BeeJees. A → B
19. There **were** four great big slashes on his forearm. A = B
    "**Look** at this, man. (A) → B
    That cat *attacked* me when I was baking a blueberry pie! A → B
    I **was** almost killed, man!" A = B
20. "George, **watch** out!" A↩

p.16

21. **Ed shouted** just in time for George to dodge the cat's jump from behind. A↻

22. **The cat soared** through the air, a few inches below the cherry pie in George's hand. A↻

    The cat landed and **turned** back in a very angry motion.
    A↻ and (A) ↻

    George looked at the cat and **gulped**. A→B and (A) ↻

    "Oh-oh... **He's gonna kill** me now." A＝B

    "George, RUN!" **everybody yelled** together. A→B

    George was already **running**, the cat right behind him in full speed. A＝B

23. **The two dashed** through the kitchen and **went** running down Ghost Avenue as **everybody laughed** behind.
    A↻ and (A) ↻ as A↻

    Ed laughed too, holding a fresh-baked country cheesecake in his hand. A↻

24. **It had been** a long month. A＝B
    A long month on Ghost Avenue. 不完全な文

p.17

25. **It had** all **begun** as a simple joke. A↻

26. **George, who used to be a handyman, had made** Ed **a sign** that said "Ed's Magic Pie Shop." A→B／B'

27. **The sign was** a token of appreciation for the pies that Ed baked for the people in the cinema. A＝B

    Ed had hung it happily In front of the cinema without much thought. A→B

28. But **the other homeless residents of Ghost Avenue who had heard stories about free pie, saw** the sign and **came** in to get some for themselves. A→B and (A) ↻

29. **Some of them** even **left** a few dimes and nickels. A→B

    George soon **found** an old deserted trailer at the northern end of Ghost Avenue and **had painted** it with leftover paint. A→B and (A) →B

    The trailer was just the right size to create a small kitchen space, so Ed **moved** his outdoor kitchen there.
    A＝B, so A→B

30. **As the days went by, more and more people started** to come buy pies, and **not all of them were** homeless.
    A→B, and A＝B

    A few curious passing cars **started** to stop by, and **several kind women who lived nearby had come** to buy a slice of pie in the spirit of charity. A→B, and A↻

21.just in time 以下は同時に起きたことを表す「時間」の付録。"dodge ball"というゲームは「ボールをよける」ゲームです。

22.1inch は 2.54cm。猫はチェリー・パイのすぐ下を通過中。

23.The two はジョージと猫。as 以下は同時に起こっていることを表す「時間」の付録。

24.It はエドがゴースト・アベニューで生活し始めてから現在までの「時間」の代役。

25.「それはすべて始まった」。何が始まったかというと、この文で始まる一連の回想シーンです。

26.that 以下は sign の化粧文。

27.token of appreciation で「感謝の印」。パイショップの看板はジョージがパイのお礼としてエドに作ってあげたものです。

28.who からカンマまでは化粧文なので、とばしてもだいじょうぶです。free pie は free hand と同じく「自由なパイ」転じて「無料のパイ」。get some の後ろには pie が省略されています。

29.them は前文の「ホームレスたち」の代役です。

30.As からカンマまでは「時間」の付録。後半の them は、パイを買いに来た more and more people の代役。

ビッグ・ファット・キャットの三色辞典

31. **They returned** for more when they found out the pies were actually good. A⤺

32. Now **the cat was** coming back down the street. A＝B
33. **The cat's whiskers were** covered with something red. A＝B
    It pretty much **suggested** the fate of the cherry pie. A→B
34. **George came** around the corner after the cat, covered with the rest of the cherry pie. A⤺
35. **Ed smiled** in spite of losing another pie. A⤺
36. **The others laughed** in an uproar. A⤺
37. **They laughed** so hard that **Ed didn't realize** Paddy was shouting. A⤺ that A→B
    "E-Ed!!" 不完全な文
    Ed finally **heard** Paddy **calling him** on the third shout and **waved** a hand at him. A→B＝B' and (A)→B
    "Sorry, Pad. **Be** back in a minute!" 不完全な文 (A)＝B
    "N-No, Ed!! 不完全な文
    You need to come back, n-now!" A→B
    Ed's smile faded when he saw that the crowd in front of the shop had grown. A⤺
38. Grown a lot. 不完全な文
    He stood there in awe, his heart beating faster and faster. A⤺
39. **He knew** something had gone wrong. A→B

    Jeremy Lightfoot Jr. **was** afraid of his father. A＝B
40. **He had** always **been** afraid of him, even as a small child. A＝B
41. **He felt** that his father was always disappointed with him, and therefore, always angry. A→B
    He never **knew** his mother. A→B
    There was nobody to protect him from his father when he was a child. A＝B
    So **he tried** desperately to be a good son. A→B
    He tried and **tried**, but nevertheless **his father was** always angry. A⤺ and (A)⤺, but A＝B
42. Now, as he stood at the door to his father's study, **his hands were** shaking. A＝B
    Jeremy **would be** thirty-one years old this year, but **he** still **felt** like a ten-year-old boy. A＝B, but A⤺

---

31. for は「ために」。more の後ろには pies が省略されています。

32. Now という単語をもって、回想シーンは終わりを告げます。ここからは現在のシーンです。

33. red は何の色？答えは次の文に。

34. ジョージの方は全身にその red をかぶっています。

35. spite はもともと「悪意」を表す単語ですが、現代ではほとんど単独では使われず、in spite of（にもかかわらず）という決まり文句の中でしか使われません。

36. The others は other people のこと。

37. 分かりにくければ that を消して、二つの文として読んでみてください。

38. Grown a lot したのは crowd。正確には The crowd had grown a lot. つまり「すごく人が増えた」。

39. had gone でぴんとこなければ、was と入れ替えてみてください。二つ先の文の had been も同様です。

40. 最初の He はジェレミー。次の him は父親。

41. この that は、彼が felt した内容を指し示しています。always angry なのはジェレミーの父親。

42. ここでも as の文が前に出ていますが、やはり「時間」の付録です。

p.17

p.18

p.19

p.20

43. **Jeremy's cat, Mr. Jones, appeared** out of nowhere and **brushed** his tail on Jeremy's foot.   A ↩ and (A) → B
    Jeremy petted Mr. Jones with a slightly trembling hand.
       A → B
    It made him **feel** a little better.   A → B = B'
    "**You wait** for me here, okay?"   A ↩

44. **Mr. Jones purred.**   A ↩
    Jeremy straightened his collar and tie and **took** a deep **breath.**   A → B and (A) → B

45. **He grabbed** the doorknob and after one last moment of hesitation, **turned** it.   A → B and (A) → B

46. "Sir. You asked me to..." **Jeremy said** in a shaking voice as **he stepped** inside.   A → B as A ↩
    "**Shut** the door, you moron."   A → B
    His father's cold voice filled the room.   A → B

43. nowhere「ない場所」から現れたということは、「どこからともなく」現れたということです。

44. 猫の鳴き声は3段階。小さくてかわいいものから順に purr → meow → cry。

45. after からカンマまでは「時間」の付録。ドアノブを grabbed してから turned するまでの間を表現しています。

46. to のあとに言えずじまいだったのは come to your office です。

p.21

Jeremy closed the door and **stood** nervously beside it.
   A → B and (A) ↩
His father was watching the morning news on television and **didn't** even **look** back.   A = B and (A) ↩
The new bodyguard, **Billy Bob, was** standing at the far wall.
   A = B
Jeremy didn't know why his father had hired Billy Bob.
   A → B
He already **had** two-dozen bodyguards around the house.
   A → B
But his **father had told** him Billy Bob was different.
   A → B／B'

47. And he **was**.   A = (B)
    Jeremy had felt it since the first time he had seen the man.
       A → B

48. There **was** a true coldness in the way Billy Bob moved.   A = B
    And he almost **never talked.**   A ↩

47. ここでの he は Billy Bob です。was の後ろに省略されているのは different。「ちがっている」ことを表す言葉でも、unique なら良い意味、different なら中立的、weird だったら悪い意味というように、イメージが少しずつ変わります。

48. the way Billy Bob moved は「彼の動く道」、転じて「彼の動き方」。

49. sense は「感覚」。ジェレミーはちょっと安心して一歩前に出ます。

p.22

"How is your business?" **Jeremy's father asked** suddenly.
   A → B
Jeremy was surprised.   A = B
His father almost **never asked** him anything.   A → B／B'

49. Feeling a sense of relief, **Jeremy took** a step forward.   A → B
50. "Great, sir. **Zombie Pies is** really taking off.   不完全な文 A = B
51. **You should see** the numbers.   A → B
52. We're the fastest growing chain in the whole..."   A = B

50. taking off は「地面から take off する」ということで、「離陸する」。ここでは「商売繁盛」のたとえです。

51. ここでは「売り上げ」を示す数字。

52. ジェレミーは in the whole state と言おうとしたのでしょうか。

ビッグ・ファット・キャットの三色辞典

53. "Good. **Close** it down." 不完全な文 (A)→B
    Jeremy stopped on his first step, stunned in shock. A↩
    "Uh... **excuse** me?" (A)→B
    "**I said**, close down the pie shops. A→B

54. **I need** the space to promote the rehabilitation project."
    A→B
    Jeremy just **stood** there, forgetting even to breathe. A↩

55. "Did you, or did you not, hear me?" **his father demanded**, still
    not moving his eyes from the television screen. A→B

56. "I... **I can't do** that, sir. A→B
    Even if **it's** your order. A=B
    It's my shop." A=B

57. **Jeremy's voice grew** smaller and smaller. A↩
    "**The kids love** my shops. A→B
    They really love Zombie Pies." A→B

    Jeremy's father said nothing. A→B
    He was watching the television screen in silence. A=B
    The morning news was showing the top news — something
    about a government scandal in Washington. A=B

58. "Please **let** me **keep** the shops. (A)→B=B'
    I really **need** this." A→B

59. "Your so-called shops will last for maybe another six
    months," **Jeremy Lightfoot Sr. said** finally. A→B
    He **spoke** in a harsh, cold tone. A↩

60. "Then **they'll get** tired of your pies and **your shops will be**
    forgotten." A→B and A=B
    "**I'll try** harder! A↩

61. **I'll make it work**! A→B=B'
    Please **give** me a chance to..." (A)→B／B'
    "Quiet." 不完全な文
    "Father..." **Jeremy protested**. A→B
    "**I said**, shut up!" A→B
    Jeremy's father suddenly **raised** his voice. A→B
    He **leaned** forward for a closer look at the television screen.
    A↩

62. "Billy Bob, **turn** up the sound." A→B
    Billy Bob **took** out the remote control and **pushed** the
    volume switch. A→B and (A)→B

63. **The voice of a reporter boomed** out of the speaker, filling the
    quiet room with a sudden burst of excitement. A↩

p.22

53. it は Zombie Pies の代役。close down は「閉めて、つぶす」転じて店をたたむということ。

54. space とはゾンビ・パイがなくなったあとの空っぽの空間です。

55. 最初の Did you の後ろに省略されているのはあとで出てくる hear me。

56. that は Zombie Pies を close down すること。

57. 「小さく小さく成長する」というと矛盾しているようですが、ジェレミーの声がどんどん小さくなっていく様子を想像してください。

p.23

58. let の前には you が省略されています。let という矢印は、何らかの希望を「かなえさせる」という意味の言葉です。

59. another six months は「もうあと6ヶ月」。ここでの last は「存続する」という矢印として使われています。

60. they はお客さんの代役。tired はよく「疲れる」の意味で使われますが、基本的に「何かにうんざりした状態」のことです。

61. it は Zombie Pies の代役。

62. その昔、テレビのチャンネルや音量はツマミを turn して変えていました。今でもその習慣が言葉の中にだけ残っています。

63. filling 以下は「どのように」の付録。quiet room が with 以下の音で満たされました。

- 6 -

p.24

"...As you can see, a small miracle has happened here on the deserted northwest side of Everville. A↺

64. People are returning to this once well-known shopping district. A=B

    A twenty-nine-year-old man, Ed Wishbone, has started a small pie shop in the ruins of an old trailer. A→B

    This is his kitchen. A=B

65. He says that all of his utensils are fully sanitized and everything is safe and clean. A→B

66. Let's ask Mr. Wishbone himself about his pies." (A)→B／B'

67. The camera moved through the side door of the pie shop and captured a shot of Ed, all red with embarrassment to the rims of his ears. A↺ and (A)→B

    Though his father didn't notice, Jeremy opened his eyes wide when he saw Ed on the screen. A→B

68. "Do you really make these pies in that backyard? A→B

    They're really good. A=B

    Sweet... but not too sweet." 不完全な文

    "Uh... thank you." (A)→B

    "Are you thinking of entering the state pie festival this weekend?" A=B

    "Pie festival?" 不完全な文

    "The Annual State Pie Festival is held this year at the Everville Mall. A=B

    You should consider entering. A ▸B

69. The prize this year is twenty thousand dollars!" A=B

    "I... I don't know. I really..." A↺ 不完全な文

70. Ed was cut off by the loud applause of the customers outside. A=B

71. "I think your customers know." A→B

    The reporter smiled and gave Ed a wink.

    A↺ and (A)→B／B'

p.25

72. "So now you've seen it, one man's journey to save the old streets of Everville. A→B

    And from the way people are gathering, who knows? A↺

    He just might succeed. A↺

73. This is Glen Hamperton reporting from Ever..." A=B

p.26

Billy Bob turned the television off. A→B

Jeremy Senior had raised his hand in the air. A→B

---

64. this once well-known shopping district とはゴースト・アベニューのこと。

65. この that も、彼が say した内容を指し示しているものです。

66. Let's は Let us のことですが、難しければこのようにひとつの矢印として考えてもかまいません。

67. all 以下は Ed の化粧品です。

68. you は Ed の代役。

69. twenty に thousand (千の位) を表すゼロ3つをつけて、20,000ドル。

70. cut off されたのは Ed のセリフです。

71. エド自身は festival に参加するべきかどうか、よく分からないと言っていますが、お客さんたちは分かっているようです。

72. この you はテレビの前の視聴者の代役。エドに向かって話していたレポーターが今度はカメラに向き直って、テレビの向こうに語りかけています。it はカンマ以下の内容の代役。エドは勝手にゴースト・アベニューの救世主に仕立て上げられてしまいました。

73. 「○○がお伝えしました」という中継の最後をしめくくる決まり文句。

"This is bad," Jeremy's father said to Billy Bob.　A→B

74. "We can't afford having this man become any more popular than he is now."　A→B

　　"Yes sir," Billy Bob replied.　A→B

　　"As for this pie festival..." Jeremy Senior turned his armchair once more towards his son, took a deep breath, and spoke.　A→B, (A)→B, and (A)↶

75. "You might as well have that chance of yours.　A→B

　　Stop this man from winning the contest and perhaps I will reconsider the termination of your enterprise."

　　(A)→B and A→B

　　"Will... will you really..."　不完全な文

76. "Do you, or do you not, want a chance?"　A→(B), or A→B

　　"Yes, sir. I'll try my best."　不完全な文　A→B

　　"Your best is far from enough. Try harder."　A=B　(A)↶

　　That said, Jeremy Senior simply turned away towards Billy Bob.　A↶

　　"Billy Bob, come here."　A↶

　　With that, his father seemed to have forgotten he was there.　A=B

　　He could probably stand there for an hour, but his father would never notice him.　A↶, but A→B

　　Jeremy Jr. stepped silently out of the room.　A↶

　　Only Mr. Jones was waiting for him there, sitting quietly in the middle of the long, empty hallway.　A=B

　　Mr. Jones purred.　A↶

　　"It's okay," Jeremy said in a sad voice.　A→B

77. "I'm used to it. Nothing new."　A=B　不完全な文

78. Jeremy picked the cat up and held it close.

　　A→B and (A)→B

79. Its warmth was comforting in the lifeless coldness of his father's house.　A=B

　　The floor of the corridor was covered with the most expensive carpet on the market and the ceiling was decorated with golden ornaments.　A=B and A=B

80. Jeremy had lived in this huge mansion for his entire life, but had always felt lost in the seemingly endless corridors of the place.　A↶, but (A)→B

81. It looked so much like his life.　A=B

　　Fabulous, but empty.　不完全な文

---

p.26

74.he (Ed) is popular now とした上で、それよりも more popular になることをジェレミーの父親は恐れています。

75.that chance とは本編 23 ページでジェレミーが欲しがっていたあのチャンスです。

76.最初の Do you の後ろに省略されているのは want a chance。

p.27

77.it は、ジェレミーと父親のやりとり全部の代役。どうやらこういった状況はジェレミーにとって「よくあること」のようです。

78.close は矢印の形もありますが、ここでは「近くに」という意味の付録。

79.Its warmthとは、前文でジェレミーが抱き上げたものの warmth です。

80.英語での mansion は、大邸宅もしくは 1 フロアを 1 世帯が独占するような高級アパートのことです。それだけ広いところなので、lost な気分になるのも無理はありません。ただ、ジェレミーの場合、もう少し大きな意味でも felt lost しているようです。

81.ここでも looked は seemed に置き換えてかまいません。

p.28

82. "Now, *that* is something you don't see everyday," Ed said to George.   A→B
He was staring with widened eyes out of the side door of the Magic Pie Shop.   A＝B
George poked his head out from behind Ed and saw it too.
   A→B and (A)→B

83. "Damned if I'm seeing that," George muttered, nearly dropping the apple he was peeling.   A→B
The cat was eating a piece of piecrust directly from Frank's hand.   A＝B

84. If Ed, George, or anybody else tried that, the result would be one less hand.   A＝B

85. "Frank's good with animals, that's for sure," George said, shaking his head with disbelief.   A→B
"That's not an animal. That's a beast," Ed said, staring at the cat.   A→B
It glared back at him.   A↩

82. この Now も特に意味のない決まり文句です。「毎日は見られない何か」の答えは四つ先の文。確かに BFC 史上初の出来事です。

83. nearly は almost と似た意味の言葉で、「すんでのところで」を表します。

84. that は前文全体の代役。

85. Frank's は Frank is の略。that's for sure は「確かに」という意味の決まり文句です。

p.29

The sunset signaled the end of another day for the Magic Pie Shop.   A→B

86. Newly baked pies were lined on the table, ready for tomorrow.   A＝B

87. They gave off the sweet, spicy smell of hot cinnamon.   A→B
Hordes of people who had seen the news came rushing in for pies immediately after the broadcast.   A↩

88. Ed sold every single slice of pie in the shop before closing for the day.   A→B

89. "Yo, Ed. Apples done, man. What next?"   不完全な文
George tossed the last peeled apple into the water bucket and washed his hands.   A→B and (A)→B

90. "Wow. You're getting faster everyday.   A＝B
Well... maybe you can help Willy and Pad clean the ovens."
   A→B＝B'
"Sure thing," George said and went out the back door.
   A→B and (A)↩
The sun was almost down.   A＝B
Orange rays came through the doorway.   A↩
Ed whistled a tune as he knelt down below the counter to get a new bowl.   A→B as A↩

86. line は「線」や「列」を表しますが、ここでは「(線のように) 並ぶ」。

87. They は前文の pies の代役。off は「離れている状態」を指します。パイの甘いにおいが、パイを離れて空中を飛んでいく様子を思い浮かべてください。

88. 「あらゆる slice を sold した」という表現は、最後の一切れまで売り尽くしたということを表します。

89. Apples done は「リンゴは終わったよ」と気軽に言っている感じです。

90. ジョージが faster になっているのは、89 で彼がやっている「仕事」です。

p.30

"Wishbone."   不完全な文

ビッグ・ファット・キャットの三色辞典

p.30

Ed **froze** as he **got** up. A↩ as A↩

91. He **found** himself **face to face with** Jeremy Lightfoot Jr.
    A → B = B'
    He also **noticed** the big shadow **standing behind him**.
    A → B = B'
92. "I'm afraid we're closed," Ed **replied**, almost a whisper. A → B
    George and the others **were** in the backyard kitchen. A = B
    He **was** alone in the shop. A = B
    Jeremy **tossed** a flier on top of the counter. A → B
93. "**Take** it. (A) → B
94. It's the entry form for this weekend's pie contest." A = B
    Ed **remained** motionless. A → B
    "Take it, Wishbone!" Jeremy **said** abruptly. A → B
95. This **made** Ed grab the flier. A → B = B'
    "You **think** you're so good. A → B
96. **Come prove** it." (A) → B

    "I don't want to be in a contest," Ed **protested** to Jeremy.
    A → B
    "This shop **is** all I want. A = B
    Please **leave us alone**." (A) → B = B'
    Jeremy **made** a face of disgust. A → B
    "You lying coward," he **said**. A → B
    "You **would love** to win, but you're afraid you'll lose.
    A → B, but A = B
97. I **bet** you've never fought for anything in your whole life."
    A → B
    Ed **kept** his eyes **on** Billy Bob. A → B = B'
98. But Jeremy's words **echoed** in his ear. A↩
    "Wishbone! **Stop ignoring me**!" 不完全な文 (A) → B
    Jeremy's voice **rose** even higher in anger. A↩
99. He **didn't know** why he was getting so mad at this man he
    hardly knew. A → B
    He **didn't** even **know** why he had come here. A → B
    "Shop! You **call** this dump a shop!? 不完全な文 A → B = B'
    A Magic Pie Shop, huh? 不完全な文
    What **does** magic **mean** anyway!? A → B
100. **Do** you **disappear or something**?" A↩
    Jeremy **snatched** the sign of the Magic Pie Shop. A → B
101. He **threw** it on the ground and **stepped** on it.
    A → B and (A) ↩
    "You **need to**..." A → B

91.「face to face」とは文字通り、顔と顔を向き合わせた状態です。

92. we're closed は「閉店です」という決まり文句。

93. it は a flier の代役。

94. entry は「入ること」、form は「形」。entry form はパイ・フェスティバルへの参加を申し込む形式的な書類のこと。

95. This は前文のジェレミーのセリフ。

96. prove は「証明する」。前文の内容を「証明しに来い」と言っています。

p.31

97. you've は you have の略。

98. Jeremy's words とはひとつ前のジェレミーの長いセリフのことです。

99. he hardly knew は this man の化粧文。「かろうじて知っているだけの人（エド）」に対して、ジェレミーはとても腹を立てているようですが……。

100. something はあらゆる矢印の代役になっています。「消えるか何かするのか？」といったところでしょうか。ジェレミーは前文で「magic とはどういう意味だ!?」と店の名前にまで文句をつけているので、こんな発言が出てきたのでしょう。

101. it は sign の代役。ダンスの「ステップ」と言いますが、stepped は「踏む」という意味の矢印です。

p.31

Jeremy **never finished** his sentence. A→B

Ed **had** suddenly **grabbed** him by the shoulder. A→B

102. Jeremy **was** caught by surprise. A=B

103. **The man in front of him had** suddenly **become** angry. A=B

104. Jeremy **noticed** this but **couldn't understand** why.

    A→B but (A)→B

He **kept** his foot **on the sign**. A→B=B'

"What are you..." 不完全な文

105. "Take your foot off my shop!" Ed **said** in a surprisingly strong voice. A→B

"It's just a sign..." A=B

Jeremy **was** cut off again. A=B

"I said, take it off!" A→B

102. caught by surprise もよく使われる決まり文句です。surprise につかまるとは、すなわち「(突然のことに)おどろく」。

103. The man とはエドのこと。

104. this は「エドが angry な状態になっていること」。ジェレミーはそんなエドに気づいていますが、なぜそうなったのかは理解できないようで……。

p.32

Ed **shoved** Jeremy off the sign. A→B=B'

Jeremy **lost** balance and **fell** down on his back.

    A→B and (A)↩

Billy Bob's large hands **grabbed** Ed, **pulled** him over the counter and **threw** him to the ground.

    A→B, (A)→B and (A)→B

106. Ed **scrambled** over to the sign on the ground and **covered** it with the only thing he had. A↩ and (A)→B

His body. 不完全な文

107. Billy Bob **was** instantly above him, kicking him on the side of his chest. A=B

It **hurt** badly and Ed **couldn't stop** coughing. A↩ and A→B

Dust **was** flying all around him. A=B

"Hey... you **don't need** to..." A→B

Jeremy **said** to Billy Bob, but **couldn't finish**. A↩, but (A)↩

108. He **had seen** the cold, hard look on Billy Bob's face. A→B

Billy Bob **kicked** Ed a second time. A→B

109. Ed **coughed** in pain again, but **refused** to get up.

    A↩, but (A)→B

He **gritted** his teeth together to stop coughing and **looked** straight up at Jeremy. A→B and (A)→B

110. He **tasted** blood in his mouth, but **was** no longer scared.

    A→B, but (A)=B

105. 読み間違いではありません。エドにとって看板は shop そのものなのでしょう。

106. it は sign の代役。エドは「持っていた唯一のもの」で看板を守ろうとしています。それが何かは次の文に。

107. Bの箱は「場所」の付録と考えてもかまいません。him はエドの代役。

108. この look は矢印ではなく「まなざし」という意味の役者です。

109. refused は「強い拒否」を表す矢印です。

110. but 以下の文は no longer が入っているために否定の文になります。「それ以上長くは続かない」、転じて「もう～しない」。

p.33

"You're just like me," Ed **said**. A→B

Billy Bob **kicked** him again. A→B

"What?" Jeremy **cried** out. A→B

111. "Are **you** out of your mind!? A=B

111. 「正気でない」ということを「mind (精神)の外」と表現しています。

112. **I'm exactly not like you!**　A = B

　　I'm rich, I'm smart, I'm... rich, I'm..."

　　　　A = B, A = B, A = B, A = ...

113. **"You don't know what a pie is made of."**　A→B

114. **Jeremy tried** hard **to laugh** but **did not succeed.**

　　　　A→B but (A) ↩

　　He shouted desperately at Billy Bob.　A↩

　　"This man is out of his mind.　A = B

　　You kicked him too much!"　A→B

　　Ed smiled.　A↩

115. **This angered Jeremy** even more.　A→B

　　He cried out.　A↩

116. **"What do you know!?"**　A→B

　　What the fuck **do you know!?"**　A→B

　　Billy Bob raised his foot over Ed's head.　A→B

　　Ed squeezed his eyes shut.　A→B

117. **But before Billy Bob could bring** his foot down, **a flash of red**

　　　flew through the air.　A↩

　　Billy Bob took a step back.　A→B

118. **Jeremy let** out **a cry** of surprise at the same time.　A→B

　　"What..."　不完全な文

　　Ed opened his eyes and **looked** up.　A→B and (A) ↩

　　Pies were flying through the air!　A = B

119. **Jeremy** frantically **wiped** hot pie from his face, but as he was

　　　doing this, **some got** in his mouth.　A→B, but, A↩

　　He stopped in silence.　A↩

　　Several pies hit him but **he didn't seem to notice.**

　　　　A→B but A = B

　　He just **looked** straight at Ed.　A→B

　　Billy Bob had mopped the pie off of his chest and **was**

　　　coming back at Ed.　A→B and (A) = B

120. **But this time, Jeremy shot** his hand out in front of Billy Bob

　　　and **stopped** him.　A→B and (A)→B

　　"That's enough," Jeremy said to Billy Bob.　A→B

　　Jeremy and Ed looked at each other one last time.　A→B

121. **The pies had** also **stopped** (probably out of ammunition).

　　　　A↩

　　"See you at the contest," Jeremy said.　A→B

　　Jeremy straightened his tie and **walked** off silently.

　　　　A→B and (A) ↩

122. **Billy Bob,** after a moment of hesitation, **followed.**　A↩

---

p.33

112. ここで exactly を使うのは本当は反則です（詳しくは解説 76 ページ）。

113. 本来は a pie is made of what. 「パイが何でできているか」。

114. 懸命に laugh しようとしたのですが、succeed しなかったようです。

115. This は前文全体の代役。

116. エドに対して、「お前が何を知っているというんだ!?」とジェレミーが詰め寄っています。

117. before からカンマまでのフレーズは「時間」の付録ですが、その中を色分けするとこうなります。Billy Bob could bring his foot down. a flash of red の正体は本編 34 ページの挿絵でジェレミーの顔にはりついているものです。

p.35

118. ジェレミーはおどろきの叫びを体の外（out）に出しました。

119. this は、ジェレミーが顔についたパイをぬぐう動作の代役。some got in his mouth は、投げつけられたパイのうち、「いくらかは口に入った」。

120. him は Billy Bob の代役。

121. 本編15ページで出てきた out of breath は「息切れ」でしたが、out of ammunition は「弾切れ」を指しています。

122. カンマからカンマまでは「時間」の付録です。本来の文は Billy Bob followed (Jeremy).

Big Fat Cat's 3 Color Dictionary

p.36

123. **When** Jeremy and Billy Bob were clearly out of sight, **George slid** down from the roof and **ran** over to Ed.
   A↺ and (A)↺

   "Ed! Man! You all right?"　不完全な文

   Ed stood up.　A↺

124. In his hands, **he held** the sign George had painted for him.
   A→B

   It was broken in half.　A＝B

   "George... **I'm sorry**."　A＝B

   "Hey man, **it's** just a sign.　A＝B

125. **I'll paint** you another one tomorrow."　A→B／B'

126. **George laughed** as if nothing had happened.　A↺

127. **It was** such a light-hearted laugh that **Ed smiled** a little too.
   A＝B that A↺

128. "Magic **ain't** in the sign, man.　A＝B

   Cheer up! **We won**!"　(A)↺ A↺

129. With that, Paddy and Willy **let** out a great big cheer of victory from the roof of the trailer.　A→B

130. **George patted** Ed on the back.　A→B

   Ed gradually **began** to laugh out loud too.　A→B

   Everyone was laughing except for the cat.　A＝B

131. **It** just **happened to come** around the shop at that moment and **was confronting** the most shocking scene of its life.
   A→B and (A)＝B

p.37

Midnight.　不完全な文

A few hours later, the "ghosts" of Ghost Avenue **were** safely **gathered** around the fire inside the cinema.　A＝B

Ed had pretty much **recovered** and **was** now **mixing** ingredients for his new pie.　A↺ and (A)＝B

132. **Everybody watched** with curiosity as **Ed took** out a jar of pickles.　A↺ as A→B

   A look of doubt **crossed** their faces as **Ed minced** the pickles and **threw** them into the bowl.　A→B as A→B and (A)→B

133. But **they managed** to remain quiet while Ed added ingredients such as boiled eggs, grated cheese, and spinach.　A→B

   When Ed reached for the small yellow bottle, however, **Willy** finally **spoke** out.　A↺

   "Ed! That's mustard," **Willy cried** as **Ed poured** mustard from the bottle into the bowl.　A→B as A→B

123.When からカンマまでは「時間」の付録。out of sight は「視界の外」。

124.George 以下は the sign の化粧文。

125.one は sign の代役。

126.as if 以下は「何も起こらなかったかのように」。

127.分かりにくければ that を消して、二つの文として読んでみてください。light-hearted laugh は「心の軽やかな笑い」。とても気持ちの良い笑いです。

128.ain't は isn't と同じです。少しやぼったい言い方です。「魔法は看板の中にはない」ということは……？

129.that はその前のジョージのセリフ全体の代役。

130.back はエドの「後ろ」、転じて「背中」。

131.It は猫の代役。「ハプニング」とも言うように、happened は「偶然起きた」ことを表す矢印です。猫にとって最もショッキングな光景とは……。

132.pickles はハンバーガーの間にはさんである、すっぱいキュウリの薄切りです。

133.they はエド以外の人たちの代役。such 以下は ingredients の具体的な内容です。

134.**Ed heard**, but **continued to pour** the yellow liquid until he had mixed the last drop into the recipe. A↰, but (A)→B
　Everybody watched with sour faces. A↰
135.**Ed looked** around the table, **saw** the faces, and **said** with a smile, "It's okay. It's my new pie."
　A→B, (A)→B, and (A)→B
　"Ed. That's mustard," **Willy repeated** simply. A→B

　"Of course, **it's** mustard. A＝B
　It's a mustard pie." A＝B
136.**This caused** everybody **to grimace**. A→B＝B'
137."It's not that bad," **Ed** quickly **added**. A→B
　Everyone replied with groans and deep sighs. A↰
　Ed, a little frustrated, **took** a freshly baked pie from under the table and **placed** it in front of everybody.
　A→B and (A)→B
138."Here. I **baked** one earlier today. 不完全な文 A→B
139.**Have** a taste." (A)→B
　Everyone took a step back from the table. A→B
　A faint smell of mustard **was** mixed with the crisp smell of piecrust. A＝B
　"Go ahead. Have a taste," **Ed insisted**. A→B
140.**The men looked** at each other hopefully, but **no one volunteered**. A→B, but A↰
　Reluctantly, **they played** a game of scissors-paper-stone to decide. A→B
　Willy lost. A↰
141.**Willy turned** towards the pie with a sad look and **found** Ed twitching his eyebrows at him. A→B and (A)→B＝B'
　He **smiled** quickly. A↰
　"Uh, Ed. **I'm happy** to have the honor of participating in this... this science experiment." 不完全な文 A＝B
　"**It's** not an experiment," **Ed said**. A→B

142."Oh, **I'm sure** that my sacrifice **will** someday **be useful** to the further development of mankind. A＝B that A＝B
143.**Well, so long everybody**." 不完全な文
　Willy waved his hand and **picked** up a piece of the mustard pie. A→B and (A)→B
　He raised it to his nose and **smelled** it. A→B and (A)→B
144.**Everyone held** their breath. A→B

134.エドが heard したのはひとつ前のウィリーのセリフ。

135.faces はエド以外の人たちの顔です。

136.This は直前のエドのセリフ全体の代役。

137.that bad とは「みんなが grimace する」ほどに bad ということ。ここではそれを否定しています。

138.one は a mustard pie の代役。

139.taste は味。「味をひとつ取れ」で「味見をしろ」。

140.hopefully は「きっと誰かが味見を買って出てくれるだろう」という hope でしたが、マスタード・パイを味見する度胸のある人はいませんでした。

141.エドにまゆをピクピクされた相手はウィリー。

142.useful の ful は「いっぱいの状態」を示す full からきています。「満タンまで use できる」が転じて「役に立つ」。

143.so long は「(皆の幸せが) so long でありますように」という意味の決まり文句で、good-bye の意。

144.「息をつかむ」は、ぐっと息を押し殺している様子。

p.39

After a moment, **Willy** **collapsed** to the floor.   A↩

145. **The others** **burst** out laughing.   A → B

"The smell!? Just with the smell!? No way!!" **Ed** **shouted**.

   A → B

146. By this time, **George, Paddy and Frank** **were** all laughing so hard that **they** **could** hardly **keep** standing.

   A = B that A → B

147. **"I'm telling you! It's not** that bad!"   A = B A = B

Ed **was** angry and **the others** **were** busy laughing.

   A = B and A = B

148. **No one except BeeJees** **realized** that Willy had fallen down awkwardly.   A → B

149. **BeeJees** **leaned** over the table to whisper to Willy, who was still lying on the floor.   A↩

p.40

"Hey, Willy. **You** **can get** up now.   不完全な文 A↩

150. **We** **got** your point. Willy?"   A → B 不完全な文

151. **BeeJees's face** **turned** white when he saw that Willy was lying face down.   A↩

152. "No! **It's not** the pie!   不完全な文 A = B

153. **It's his heart! It's doing** it again!"   A = B A = B

BeeJees **jumped** across the table to Willy.   A↩

The others **were** still laughing.   A = B

"What?" **Ed** **asked**.   A → B

He **could not hear** what BeeJees had said because of the laughter.   A → B

But **everyone** **stopped** laughing when BeeJees held up Willy's limp body.   A → B

154. "Prof! C'mon! Prof!"   不完全な文

Ed froze.   A↩

He couldn't understand what was happening.   A → B

He cried out in almost sheer panic.   A↩

"BeeJees! **What** the hell **is going** on!?"   不完全な文 A = B

"Don't worry. It's not your pie," **BeeJees** **turned** back and **replied** quickly.   A↩ and (A) → B

Sweat **was running** down his forehead.   A = B

"**Willy's heart** **is** in a real bad condition."   A = B

All Ed could say was, "Why isn't he in a hospital?"   A = B

155. "Because **hospitals cost** money."   A → B

156. "**Use** mine."   (A) → B

Ed **took** his wallet out instantly and **held** it out to BeeJees.

   A → B and (A) → B

---

145. さっきまでの緊張が解けて、笑いが burst out (破裂する) しました。

146. they はジョージ、パディ、フランクの代役。彼らは standing の状態を保っているのがやっとというほど笑っています。

147. この that bad とは「ウィリーが倒れる」ほどに bad。

148. ビージーズ以外に that 以下のことを realized した人はいませんでした。

149. who 以下は Willy の化粧文。

150. 「いかにそのパイがひどいものであるか」という point について「よく分かった」ということ。

151. that はビージーズが見たものを指し示しています。

152. みんなが「パイのせいだろう」と思っているので、「そうじゃない!」とビージーズ。

153. 後半の文の最初の It は his heart の代役。二つ目の it は、はっきりとは分かりませんが、「心臓がまたあれをやった」というニュアンスから想像してみてください。

154. Prof は Professor の略。でも、ふつうはこのように略して呼ぶことはありません。

155. 矢印としての cost は「(費用が) かかる」という意味。

156. mine は my money のこと。

A cold feeling was rising up in his heart.   A = B
Willy wasn't moving.   A = B
157. His mouth was half open, as if he had stopped breathing.
   A = B
   Grasping the situation at last, George and Paddy rushed over to Willy and started slapping his face.
   A↩ and (A) → B
   The night suddenly seemed a lot darker and colder.   A = B
158. "Hospital costs lots of money. At least two grand a week. And that's without any treatment," BeeJees said to Ed as he was giving CPR to Willy.   A → B
   "He's not responding!" Paddy cried out, almost in tears.
   A → B
   "Oh no.. This is bad, man. This is really bad."   A = B A = B
   George was sweating hard too.   A = B
159. This was the first time Ed had seen George with a serious face.   A = B
   But Ed still couldn't move.   A↩
   All he could do was stand there and ask in a dumbfounded voice, "Isn't there a phone somewhere? We need an ambulance."   A = B
160. "You know there isn't a single working phone on this street," BeeJees said to Ed.   A → B
161. He was angry.   A = B
   Probably not angry at Ed, but angry.   不完全な文
   BeeJees took a deep breath, trying to calm down.   A → B
   "Besides..., no ambulance would come here at this time of night."   A↩
   "Then what are we supposed to do?   A = B
162. He's dying, isn't he?"   A = B
   "Pray," BeeJees answered.   A → B

   BeeJees, George, and Paddy were trying to do everything they could.   A = B
163. But anybody could see this wasn't enough.   A → B
   Ed looked desperately around the theater and found a rusty shopping cart by the wall.   A → B and (A) → B
164. He grabbed the cart and a few old blankets and hurried over to Willy.   A → B and (A) ↩
165. "We have to get him to a hospital."   A → B

p.40

157. 本編 36 ページなどに登場した as if が再び出てきました。as if 以下の文は限りなく現実に近い架空の話。「息を止めてしまったかのように」。

158. セリフの中の that は two grand の代役。「何の治療もなく（入院するだけで）2,000 ドル」と言っています。CPR とは cardiopulmonary resuscitation の略で心臓マッサージのこと。

p.41

159. Ed 以下は the first time の化粧文。ジョージのシリアスな顔がよほど珍しかったのでしょう。

160. 仕事をしている電話＝使える電話。

161. He はビージーズの代役。

162. dying は「死んでいる」ではなく、「死にかけている」。完全に死んでいるなら He's dead.

163. this は前文全体の代役で、できる限りのことをしようとしていたが、「十分でなかった」と示しています。

164. 矢印のあとに over がつくと、ただ hurried to Willy とするよりも、間にあるものを飛びこえて行ったような「勢い」が加わります。

165. 「彼を病院に連れていくことを（予定の中に）持っている」、つまり「連れていかねばならない」。

p.42

p.42

Ed **reached** for Willy's hand but BeeJees **slapped** his arm away.　A→B but A→B

"Don't!"　不完全な文

"Why not!? For heaven's sake!"　不完全な文

"He **wanted** to die, Wishbone.　A→B

166. If he's going to die, **let** him **die** here."　(A)→B=B'

"That's insane!"　A=B

167. "Wishbone.　You're just **making** this harder.　不完全な文

　A=B

168. **Let** him **go**."　(A)→B=B'

Ed **reached** for Willy again.　A→B

BeeJees **started** to stop him, but this time, Ed **pushed** him away and **said** to George, "C'mon and help me.　We have to get him to a hospital."　A→B, but, A→B and (A)→B

George **nodded** and **started** helping Ed wrap Willy in one of the blankets.　A↩ and (A)→B

Together, they **carried** Willy over to the shopping cart.　A→B

BeeJees just **sat** there on the ground shaking his head.　A↩

"I'm **telling** you, Wishbone.　A=B

You're just increasing everyone's pain."　A=B

166. let の前に省略されているのは you。「彼がここで死ぬことをかなえさせてやる」、転じて「ここで死なせてやろう」。

167. this はこの状況全体を指す代役。

168. どこへ行くのかというと「天国」。日本語の「逝く」と似た表現です。

p.43

Ed **finished** tucking Willy into the blanket and **turned** back to BeeJees.　A→B and (A)↩

He **was scared**.　A=B

169. **Part** of him **knew** that BeeJees was probably right.　A→B

170. But another **part** of him, the warmer, stronger part of him **spoke**.　A↩

"I **know** I'm naive.　A→B

I just **don't want** to give up.　A→B

I've **given** up too many things already."　A→B

The shopping cart **flew** through the theater doors, Ed and George pushing it from behind.　A↩

BeeJees **watched** the doors swing from the force of the passing shopping cart.　A→B=B'

171. He **knew** what was going to happen.　A→B

He **slumped** to the ground, biting his lower lip as the tears **came**, one by one, down his dry cheek.　A↩ as A↩

"**Damn** it, Wishbone.　(A)→B

Why **can't** you **understand**?　A↩

It's too late.　We're all too late."　A=B　A=B

169. him はエドの代役。「エドの中のある部分」。

170. another part は、前文を受けた「それ以外の部分」。

171. He はビージーズの代役。彼はこの時すでに、病院に行ってもどうなるか知っていました。

- 17 -

ビッグ・ファット・キャットの三色辞典

The night outside was cold and quiet. A = B
The moon was almost full, with a perfect sky behind it — no clouds at all. A = B
172. There was no one in sight. A = B
173. A car passed every once in a while, but other than that, everything was silent except for the rattle of their shopping cart. A↻, but , A = B
Ed and George pushed the cart down Ghost Avenue until they came to the intersection of Lake Every Drive. A → B
174. They crossed the intersection carefully and continued walking south. A → B and (A) → B
175. The hospital was about a mile further down the road. A = B
176. It had been easy until then. A = B
But when they entered the downtown district, the road changed uphill. A↻
It was not a steep incline. A = B
177. Perhaps you wouldn't notice it if you were walking. A → B
But it made a pretty big difference if you were a child or a jogger — or even two men pushing a shopping cart. A → B

The rattle of the rusted cart suddenly broke off when one of the front wheels snapped free. A↻
178. The cart was forced to a stop. A = B
Ed knelt down and examined the broken wheel.
　A↻ and (A) → B
George came over to Ed and whispered to him, "No way we can repair this." A↻ and (A) → B
George was right. A = B
A sense of unease filled Ed as he said, "I guess we'll have to carry the cart." A → B as A → B
"Maybe I can carry Willy on my back," George suggested.
　A → B
179. "It... might not be a good idea to rock him too much. A = B
180. Besides we still have a mile to go. A → B
181. Can you take the front end? A → B
182. I'll get the back." A → B
"No problem." 不完全な文
George nodded. A↻
And so they went. A↻
Two shadows in the moonlight carrying a man in a shopping cart. 不完全な文

p.44

172.本編 36 ページの out of sight に対して、今度は in sight で「視界の中に」。この場合の one は「人」です。no one なので「誰もいない」状態になります。

173. once in a while は「ある期間に 1 回」、つまり「時々」。that は A car から最初のカンマまでを指しています。

174. south は「場所」の付録で、「南へ」。

175. about は「おおよそ」を示す接着剤。病院はこの道のさらに先 (further)、1 マイルぐらいのところにあります。

176. then は今この時。

177. 本編 7-11 ページの you と同じく、ここでの you は読者の「あなた」を指しています。it は the road が uphill に変化したということの代役。

p.45

178. forced は強い力を表す言葉で、「stop することを強いた」。

179. It は後半の to 以下の代役。him はウィリーを指します。rock は体を激しくゆさぶることで、音楽のジャンル名にもなっているあのロックです。

180. to go は a mile の化粧品。

181. front end はカートの「前の終わり」転じて、「前の端」。

182. 前文の front に対して、「back を持とう」とエドが申し出ています。

183. **Sweat rolled** down Ed's face, although **the first hundred steps were** not hard.   A↺, although A = B

184. But after ten minutes, **the weight of the cart started** to feel like the weight of a small car.   A→B

Ed's arms and feet were getting weaker and weaker by the moment.   A = B

Ed glanced back over his shoulder.   A↺

185. **He shouldn't have.**   A↺

186. **Fear ran** through him as **he realized** that they still had more than half way to go.   A↺ as A→B

The hospital was a small red glow at the top of the hill.   A = B

187. **It wasn't** that far, but **it seemed** miles away.   A = B, but A = B

188. **The only thing that kept Ed moving was** Willy's lifeless face lying within the pile of musty blankets.   A = B

He had to keep walking.   A→B

He had to.   A→B

*Son. **You are** a baker.*   不完全な文   A = B

189. **Professor Willy was** the first person who had ever called him a baker.   A = B

He would never forget that.   A→B

190. **He would never,** ever **forget** that.   A→B

191. One at a time, **he took** careful steps forward.   A→B

His legs were weak now.   A = B

192. One wrong step and **he might lose** balance.   A→B

193. As they passed the elementary school, **Ed thought** he heard someone say something in a really soft voice.   A→B

He thought that maybe George was saying something to encourage himself.   A→B

194. But **it wasn't** George.   A = B

195. **He could see** that, even from behind.   A→B

Then who —   不完全な文

"Willy?" **Ed said.**   A→B

George stopped and **looked** back.   A↺ and (A)↺

Willy's mouth was moving slightly.   A = B

Ed leaned forward and **listened** carefully.   A↺ and (A)↺

At first, **he thought** Willy was just breathing.   A→B

But then **he was** able to hear the soft sounds coming from Willy's mouth.   A = B

---

p.45

183. first step は「最初の一歩」。hundred が入れば「最初の百歩」。

184.「カートの重さは like 以下のように感じられ始めた」。

185. 補うと、He shouldn't have glanced back. shouldn't は「するべきではなかった」。

186. to go が分かりにくければ、とばして読んでみてください。

187. that far は前の文で見えたほどには far ではないということ。

p.46

188. Ed を moving の状態に保ち続けた only thing が B の箱の中身です。

189. who 以下は、the first person につく化粧文。him はエドの代役。

190. ever は never をさらに強調しています。never ever は決まり文句です。

191. One at a time は「ひとつずつ」という決まり文句。

192. and をはさんで、もし左側が起きたら右側になるとしています。

193. B の箱の中を色分けすると、he heard someone say something in a really soft voice. A→B = B' となります。

194. この it は「soft voice の主」の代役。

p.47

195. that は前文全体の代役。

"He's... singing," **Ed said** to George with an amazed look.
 A→B

"Singing?" **George gasped** and **listened**.   A→B and (A) ↺

"Oh, yeah. **I hear** it too."   不完全な文   A→B

It was such a soft and tender voice.   A＝B

196.**Ed and George started** to walk again, but somehow **it was**
 easier this time.   A→B, but A＝B

 The hospital seemed closer and **the cart seemed** lighter.
 A＝B and A＝B

 Ed noticed the full moon in the sky for the first time.   A→B

 And in spite of all the chaos, **it was** still beautiful.   A＝B

197.**A comfortable breeze circled** around them.   A↺

198.**George began** to sing along with Willy.   A→B

199.**It was** a song Ed had heard millions of times, but **he had**
 never realized how beautiful it was until now.
 A＝B, but A→B

 Tears formed in his eyes.   A↺

200.**There were** so many things he still had to learn.   A＝B

 The world was so huge and so full of surprises.   A＝B

 The world is not a mustard pie, Ed.   A＝B

201.No, **it wasn't**.   A＝(B)

 Ed closed his eyes and **listened** to Willy and George singing.
 A→B and (A)→B

 And after a moment, **he** too, **joined** the song.   A→B

Door.   不完全な文
Emergency.   不完全な文
Get help.   (A)→B

202.**These were** the only thoughts left in Ed's head when they
 finally reached the emergency entrance of the Everville
 Hospital.   A＝B

 He somehow **found** some final dregs of strength in his legs
 and **wobbled** up to the doors.   A→B and (A) ↺

 They were locked.   A＝B

 Ed banged his fist on the doors.   A→B

 "Someone! **Someone, help** us!   不完全な文   A→B

 We need help!"   A→B

 The lights were dark inside.   A＝B

 Nobody answered Ed's call.   A→B

203.**Ed took** a quick look at the shopping cart.   A→B

 Willy had stopped singing and **was** as quiet as before.
 A→B and (A)＝B

196.it は「(cart をかついで) walk すること」の代役。

197.circle は「円」を表す役者ですが、ここでは「円を描く」という矢印。

198.along 以下は「どのように」の付録。

199.Ed からカンマまでは a song の化粧文です。後半の it は a song の代役。

200.he以下はsomany things の化粧文で、「学ぶことを予定の中に持っている」、転じて「学ばなければならない」。

201.it は The world の代役。一見否定の文に見えますが、前文の「世界はマスタード・パイではない」というのを受けて、「(確かに)そうではなかった」と言っています。

202.These は直前の三つの文の代役。left in Ed's head は thoughts (考え) の化粧文です。

203.「エドは素早いまなざしを一回 took した」転じて「エドは素早く見た」。

204. **George was** totally exhausted and **was down** on his hands
 and knees.　A = B and (A) = B
 Ed wanted to give up and lie down too, but **he continued to**
 hit the door.　A→B, but A→B
 Then suddenly, **the sound of a window opening came** from
 above.　A↩

 Ed backed away a few steps and **found a nurse looking**
 down at them suspiciously.　A↩ and (A)→B = B'
 "Ma'am, we need help," **Ed said.**　A→B
205. **The nurse didn't answer**, but **her eyes studied** Ed and the
 others carefully — their dirty ripped clothing, Willy's
 long beard, and the rusted old shopping cart.
 　A↩, but A→B
 "Please. **We need a doctor.**　不完全な文　A→B
206. If it's money, **I have some.**　A→B
207. And **I promise** I'll get more in a few days."　A→B
 The nurse started to close the windows.　A→B
208. "No! Please! We really need help! Here!" **Ed shouted**
 desperately as **he emptied** his wallet on the sidewalk.
 　A→B as A→B
 He scattered small change and a few dollar bills around him.
 　A→B
 "**This is** all the money I have now, but...!!"　A = B
209. **The window closed** shut with a cold sound.　A↩
210. **Ed was left** in the dark with only silence for an answer.　A = B
 "Please... we..."　不完全な文
 Ed's voice faded as **he slumped** down on the ground.
 　A↩ as A↩

 George crawled over to Ed and **put** his hands on Ed's
 shoulders.　A↩ and (A)→B
211. Looking at George's face, **Ed realized** that George had
 known this would happen.　A→B
 But **he had helped** him anyway.　A→B
 "At least **we tried**, man."　A↩
 George smiled.　A↩
 It was a true smile.　A = B
 "I bet the Prof's happy too."　A→B
 Yo, man. Maybe it's time to give up.　不完全な文　A = B
 Leave things to good old Jesus upstairs."　(A)→B

204. hands and knees が地面に on（接触）しているので、四つんばいになっています。

205. ここでの studied は「勉強する」というよりも「観察する」。nurse が観察しているのは彼らの外見です。

206. あえて言うなら it は「あなたの必要なもの」の代役です。「お金ならある」という言いにくいことを言おうとしているので、やわらげた表現を使っています。

207. more の後ろには money が省略されています。

208. as 以下の行動と同時にエドは叫んでいます。

209. closed と shut はどちらも「閉じる」という意味ですが、closed がふつうに閉めているのに対して、shut はピシャッと音をたてて閉める感じです。この文では closed が矢印なので、shut は「どのように」の付録として使われています。

210. silence だけがエドに対しての answer でした。

211. this はこの状況全体の代役。ジョージもこうなるのは分かっていました。

ビッグ・ファット・キャットの三色辞典

p.52

Ed sat still on the concrete.　A↶

He knew George was right.　A→B

212.Just as BeeJees **had been** right all along.　A＝B

　　Ed gripped his thighs and **lowered** his head close to the ground.　A→B and (A)→B

213.**He felt** hope **running out of him**.　A→B＝B'

　　He knew he was about to give up.　A→B

214.**Ed had** almost **never prayed** in his life, but at that moment, he **prayed** from the bottom of his heart.　A↶, but, A↶

　　He prayed for courage.　A→B

215.The courage not to give up.　不完全な文

212.Just as は「同じように」という意味。この一文は前の文についての「どのように」の付録としてとらえられます。

213.エドは hope が流れ出ていくように感じました。

214.bottom は「底」。bottom of his heart で「心の底」。

p.53

"Yo, c'mon Ed," George **called**.　A→B

As Ed was getting up, something **fell** out of his chest pocket.　A↶

It **floated** in the air for a moment, then **landed** silently on the ground.　A↶, (A)↶

Ed picked it up.　A→B

"Yo. **Let's go** home.　不完全な文 (A)↶

I think Willy's just sleeping.　A→B

He'll be fine until tomorrow morning."　A＝B

216.George **caught** Ed under the arm and **helped** him to his feet.　A→B and (A)→B＝B'

　　Ed was still holding the flier.　A＝B

217.His eyes **were glued** to the words printed on it.　A＝B

218.As he read those words, something Willy had said to him a while before **circled** around his mind.　A↶

　　Ed. Willy had said.　不完全な文 A↶

　　You are a baker.　A＝B

　　You are a baker.　A＝B

　　You are a baker.　A＝B

215.前文の courage を具体的に説明しています。「give up しない勇気」。

216.him はエドの代役。「エドが足につくのを助けた」、転じて「エドが立ち上がるのを助けた」。

217.it は the flier の代役。

218.Willy から before までは something の化粧文です。

p.54

ビッグ・ファット・キャットの三色辞典
～マジック・パイ・ショップ編～

三色辞典の使い方

赤い色は **A** の箱
緑の色は →、↰ または ＝
青い色は **B** の箱
濃い青色は二つ目の **B'** の箱
（めったにありませんが）
色がないのは付録
そして、これが文の形

Ed gave the cat a present yesterday. A→B／B'

分かりにくい文については、ページの右側に少し詳しい解説がのっています。同じ数字のついた文と照らし合わせてご覧ください。

この三色辞典は『ビッグ・ファット・キャットの世界一簡単な英語の本』で紹介されている方法論に基づき、本編の英文を色分けして、解説を加えたヒントブックです。もちろん「答え」ではありません。考える上でのひとつのガイドラインとしてお使いください。